The Advanced
Guide:

Follow the Best Beginner Forex Trading Guide for Making Money Today! You'll Learn Secret Forex Market Strategies to the Fundamental Basics of Being a Currency Trader!

Neil Sharp

☒ Copyright 2019 by _____ All rights reserved.

The follow eBook is reproduced below with the goal of providing information that is as accurate and reliable as possible. Regardless, purchasing this eBook can be seen as consent to the fact that both the publisher and the author of this book are in no way experts on the topics discussed within and that any recommendations or suggestions that are made herein are for entertainment purposes only. Professionals should be consulted as needed prior to undertaking any of the action endorsed herein.

This declaration is deemed fair and valid by both the American Bar Association and the Committee of Publishers Association and is legally binding throughout the United States.

Furthermore, the transmission, duplication or reproduction of any of the following work including specific information will be considered an illegal act irrespective of if it is done electronically or in print. This extends to creating a secondary or tertiary copy of the work or a recorded copy and is only allowed with express written consent from the Publisher. All additional right reserved.

The information in the following pages is broadly considered to be a truthful and accurate account of facts and as such any inattention, use or misuse of the information in question by the reader will render any resulting actions solely under their purview. There are no scenarios in which the publisher or the original author of this work can be in any fashion deemed liable for any hardship or damages that may befall them after undertaking information described herein.

Additionally, the information in the following pages is intended only for informational purposes and should thus be thought of as universal. As befitting its nature, it is presented without assurance regarding its prolonged validity or interim quality. Trademarks that are mentioned are done without written consent and can in no way be considered an endorsement from the trademark holder.

Table of Contents

Introduction
Chapter 1: What is Forex Trading?
Chapter 2: The Basics of Forex Trading
Chapter 3: Forex Trading Strategies
Chapter 4: How to Enter and Exit Trades
Chapter 5: Best Options Trading Tools
Chapter 6: Preparation Prior to Market Entry
Chapter 7: Forex Charts and Forex Trade Practice
Chapter 8: Find a Broker and Open a Trading Account
Conclusion

Introduction

Congratulations on downloading this book and thank you for doing so.

The following chapters will discuss Forex trading and everything you need to learn to become a great trader. A lot of people are now earning a second stream of income through the Forex markets. If you learn how to trade Forex, then you can begin earning an attractive passive income and enjoy profits beyond what you thought possible.

Forex trading provides an excellent method of earning an additional income. This book teaches you all that you need to learn about Forex, the different currencies involved, how to buy, how to sell, and how to earn a profit. If you read all the chapters, you will understand why Forex is so profitable. In fact, the Forex market is the largest financial market in the world. Trading this market is very lucrative as long as you know what you are doing.

There are plenty of books on this subject on the market, thanks again for choosing this one! Every effort was made to ensure it is full of as much useful information as possible, please enjoy!

Chapter 1: An Introduction to Forex Trading

The term *Forex* stands for foreign exchange market and is abbreviated FX. Forex refers to the market place where different currencies are traded. A simple Forex transaction is said to take place when a person exchanges money in local currency and receives foreign currency to facilitate overseas travel. There is a huge need by people around the world to exchange currencies. Businesses and individuals trade all the time and they exchange foreign currencies in the process.

What is Forex?

The Forex market is the largest market in the entire world. It is also the most liquid financial market and generally outperforms all other financial markets in America, Europe, and all over the world. The average turnover of the Forex markets is almost $2 trillion. However, across the board, there is more than $3.2 trillion traded each day between corporations, governments, traders, and speculators. These amounts are staggering and serve as proof that the market is large enough for everyone. With such amounts at play each day, you can now understand why so many people are trading Forex on a regular basis.

There is basically no centralized platform where currencies are traded. They are traded electronically where all transactions are digitally conducted over the counter on computers spread out across the globe. Forex markets are open 24 hours a day everyday so traders can trade whenever they want and from whatever location they please.

As a trader, you stand to earn attractive returns if you engage in Forex trade. However, you need to learn as much as possible about Forex. The more you learn the better your chances of high returns. For instance, you have to understand how the Forex industry is currently mapped out. This is because market players determine how much money is available to traders. There are investment banks and hedge funds with billions of dollars available to trade while smaller traders control only a few thousand dollars.

Forex markets

The value of currencies fluctuates each and everyday. Sometimes the price is up and sometimes it is down. When we trade in currencies, we are hoping to benefit and profit from these minute but significant price movements.

One of the best known and most successful Forex traders is the billionaire George Soros. Mr. Soros made a billion dollars in a single day trading currencies. Even then Forex trading can be a risky affair and you can lose most of your money. This is the case across most financial markets so it is important to learn as much as possible about Forex trading and how to trade before starting to trade.

Technology has also improved greatly in the last couple of decades making it possible to trade online. You can now begin trading as a small trader or investor because you no longer need large amounts of money to trade the Forex markets.

As it is the Forex market is the largest financial market in the entire world. Compare its daily turnover of $3.2 trillion with that of the NYSE which is $55 billion. Even when we combine the daily output of all the world's stock markets, they only make up a quarter the size of the Forex market.

The size of the Forex market is really important. Since there are so many traders and other players, transaction costs are kept pretty low. Here are some interesting factors about Forex trading.

- Most firms in the Forex market do not charge a commission. All that you have to do is pay for the spreads.

- Since trading takes place 24 hours per day, you choose the trading times and determine how to conduct your trades

- Once you learn how to trade, you can make using leverage. This will increase your profitability immensely

- There are only limited currency pairs to choose from. This makes things easier compared to trading securities where you have over 5000 different stocks to choose from

What is traded?

Countries have their own currencies. For instance, in the US we have the US Dollar and in Canada we have the Canadian dollar. The value of any Forex currency is often a reflection of the market's opinion about the country's current and future health of the economy. Economic factors like inflation, high unemployment, and recession all have a direct effect on the strength of a sovereign currency. Forex trading therefore pits the economy of one country against that of another.

Currency pairs

Currencies are usually traded in pairs. Therefore, before trading, you will need to choose a pair to trade. The value of a particular currency against another is usually determined by the activity of the currency pairs. Take the case of the EUR or euro and the AUD or Australian dollar. When these two are paired, the movement will measure the value of euro versus that of the Australian dollar. If this value increases then it means that there has been an increase in the euro's value compared to that of the Australian dollar. The reverse is also true.

Because currencies are paired, and their values vary all the time, your aim and that of all other traders will be to benefit from the price movement.

Even small movements matter. There are several currencies that are usually paired. Basically you can pair any of the following currencies.

- USD – the US Dollar
- CHF – the Swiss Franc
- EUR – the Euro
- NZD – the New Zealand Dollar
- JPY – the Japanese Yen
- CAD – the Canadian Dollar
- GBP – the British Pound
- AUD – the Australian Dollar

The above currencies are the main Forex currencies. When you pair any of them against the US dollar, you will have a major currency pair. Examples include pairs like CAD/USD, NZD/USD and so on. Minor pairs are any pairs that do not consist of the US dollar such as CAD/AUD and so on.

Apart from the majors and minors, we also have exotic currencies. They include the Norwegian Kroner, NOK, Thai Baht, THB, South African Rand, ZAR, and the Hong Kong Dollar, HKD. An exotic currency pair is one that consists of the major currencies paired with one of the exotic currencies.

Forex trading versus Stock trading

Forex trading is vastly different from stock market trading. For starters, there is no central exchange when it comes to Forex. Traders make their trades over counters between one trader and another. They also trade through Forex dealers and brokers.

Forex traders are found all over the world. They live in different countries from Japan to China, USA and Canada, Europe and Australia, and so on. They trade across different time zones and because of this the markets are open 24 hours each working day. This is different from stock markets which are open for only a couple of hours each day.

As previously observed, currencies are traded in pairs and the prices are also quoted for currency pairs. There are regular currency fluctuations that happen frequently though in minute increments. These increments provide traders with opportunities to trade and make money off their trades. However, it is not easy to make huge returns based on small investments. This is why most traders learn how to leverage.

Advantages of Forex Trading

There are certain benefits of trading Forex compared to other forms trading. One of the main benefits of Forex trading is definitely liquidity. Forex trading is a very liquid venture and the market is also very liquid. This basically means that there are very many traders who are always buying and selling currencies. Because of this, trades are executed very fast both selling and buying hence there is always currency and profits exchanging hands. This liquidity makes the Forex market a very attractive venture for small and large investors.

Leverage

Another huge benefit of trading Forex is leverage. Most Forex brokers and agencies are often willing to lend their clients upfront money to execute trades. Leverage is basically a loan advanced to a trader by their broker. Brokers in the Forex market offer the highest leverage amounts compared to brokers in other markets.

The reason why leverage is much higher in Forex markets is because traders only require a tiny percentage of the total price of a particular position. Take a leverage of 250:1 with only $500 to invest. It is possible, using leverage, to assume a position of $125,000. If well utilized, leverage can lead to great returns.

Low entry levels

Another huge benefit of Forex trading is that entry levels are very low. This is enabled largely by the high liquidity in this particular market. Anyone with as little as $100 is able to open a brokerage account and start trading right away. This is often not the case across other financial markets where entry levels are much higher.

Low cost of transactions

Forex traders are fortunate because they are charged much lower fees by their brokers compared to other traders. The reason is because most Forex brokers usually earn their revenue via the spread. The spread refers to the difference between currency selling and buying prices. Since brokers generate their revenues from the spread and with the high volumes of trade, low fees are still profitable. This also makes it easier for most people to begin trading the markets.

Zero market manipulation

Unlike other markets, the Forex market is almost impossible to manipulate. Often in other markets such as the stocks market, some major players are able to affect prices and manipulate trade. Where markets are much smaller, a huge order from one participant or trader can largely affect prices. This is not possible on the Forex markets because this market is too large. It is 100 times larger than the New York Stock Exchange. Significant movements in Forex currencies are often as a result of government policies, reports, factors such as inflation, and global news such as war, an embargo and so on.

How exactly is Forex traded?

Trading currencies is very similar to trading stocks. In this case however, you will be buying one currency while at the same time selling another. This is the main reason why currencies are ordinarily quoted in pairs. You can have Forex quotes such as USD/AUD, EUR/JPY and so on.

Forex trading occurs instantly. This means that when you trade the trade takes place on the spot so that funds are actually exchanged instantly. Keep in mind that you are basically buying a currency while selling another all at the same time. As an example, if you see the EUR/USD Forex quoted as 1.19, this means that you need to pay $1.19 in order to buy a single euro.

Therefore, as you trade currencies you will actually be selling your dollars and use the proceeds to purchase Euros as in our case above. Also, each currency has a certain interest rate attached to it by its Central Bank.

Even then, you need not be a regular trader in order to benefit from the Forex market. Simply travelling overseas or buying products from another country will have you participate in Forex trade.

Carry trade

Another method of making money while trading currencies is carry trade. This method is popular among currency traders. It is basically a strategy where a trader borrows low-interest currencies and then uses these to invest in high-interest currencies. The aim of this approach is to earn a profit from currency trade and also hope the currency purchased will appreciate in value.

For success with carry trade you should focus both on pairing a high interest currency with a low interest one and the spread's direction. The ideal situation should be where the central bank of the currency in which you have a long outlook is seeking to increase interest rates whereas the other is expecting lower interest rates.

In brief, the aim in this instance is to identify a currency pair whose interest spread is high and is experiencing an upward trend. To implement this strategy successfully, you will require a deeper understanding of fundamentals that affect interest rates.

Eight major currencies

In the stock market, you get to choose from thousands of different stocks. However, in the Forex markets, you get to choose from only 8 major currencies which represent eight major economies of the world. These include Canada, EU, Australia, United States, Japan, New Zealand, the UK, and Switzerland.

These eight nations have some of the world's most sophisticated financial systems. When you focus mostly on these eight currencies, you can financially benefit from the currency fluctuations that happen all the time. You will also earn from the world's most liquid and creditworthy financial market.

As a trader or investor, you can access financial and economic information from any of these countries on a daily basis. This information can be used for analysis so that you can determine the best currency pair to choose from. As such, you are able to trade currencies based on sound and trustworthy information and analysis.

Interest rates

As you begin trading in currencies, you need to know that there is interest charged by various central banks. When you deal in any currency, you will be obligated to pay some interest on the currency.

Basically, you make a profit on the currency that you buy but pay interest after selling a currency.

As a trader, it is crucial that you find out the direction of interest rates. Of course there are certain factors that determine this. One of these is the size of a country's economy. Country's that register strong growth and whose economies are performing well are likely to raise interest rates in the course of the financial year.

On the other hand, countries whose economies are experiencing difficulties and performing poorly are likely to experience reduced interest rates. If you can understand how interest rates work and how they affect currencies and other related policies, then you stand a good chance of success trading currencies.

Another important point to note is that there is plenty of leverage that you can use to your benefit. Leverage sometimes gets as high as 100:1 which implies that with only $100 you can handle currencies worth a whooping $10,000. If you are an astute trader, then you can earn that much money with only $100.

A lot of successful Forex traders use leverage to earn huge profits with limited resources. You should however avoid leverage as much as possible until you have sufficient experience trading currencies as well as an understanding as to how it works.

There is some risk involved

You also need to be fully conscious of possible risks when trading currencies. This is true not just with Forex trading but with all kinds of trades because there is some risk involved. What you need to do is get some education about Forex trading, learn how to do it properly and then do a lot of practice on a demo platform. It is only through practice and understanding how Forex works that you will be able to trade safely and make attractive profits.

Chapter 2: The Basics of Trading Forex

Forex trading has become extremely popular as it provides a pathway for any keen trader to join and begin earning huge profits. Currencies are crucial to the global economy and as such are held to a certain level of importance. The reason is that they are used to facilitate foreign trade, business, travel, and much more.

There is no central exchange platform or marketplace where Forex trades are managed or overseen. Most trades are conducted and concluded on digital platforms across the internet and sometimes over the counter or OTC. As such, all trades are executed over computer networks across the entire globe.

Forex markets are available 24 hours a day, Mondays to Fridays. Traders have to sign up with a Forex brokerage firm so as to trade. They provide their services at these times. Trades occur across all the different time zones and in all major financial capitals including Sydney, Tokyo, Singapore, Paris, Zurich, New York, and London.

Forex Trading Strategies and Styles

Now that you understand the basics of Forex trade, you need to learn how to trade. There are different strategies that you can adapt when it comes to Forex. Some of these strategies and approaches are thought to be a lot more effective in comparison to others. Once you learn about these strategies, you should try them out in order to identify the one that suits you most and that you are most comfortable with.

First of all, you will come across bid and ask prices on Forex platforms. The bid price simply refers to the value or cost of a currency that you want to buy. Therefore, when you buy a currency, you will be paying the bid price. On the other hand we have the ask price. The ask price is the price at which you will sell your currency. These prices are constantly fluctuating based on the demand and supply in the market just like it happens on other markets.

- *Day trading strategy:* This is a strategy where trades are entered into and then concluded within the same day. If you set up a Forex trade via this strategy, then you will conclude it before the end of the day. The main aim of this strategy is to protect a trader from incurring overnight losses as there are events that could alter price directions of certain currencies.

- *Swing trade strategy:* This is a trading strategy that lasts between a single day and an entire week. You adapt this strategy if you have a long term outlook on certain currencies and wish to allow the strategy to mature.

- *Trading the trend strategy:* In this instance, a trader will be trading in accordance with the market trend. As such, you will follow the market trend and trade according to its movement.

There are other strategies that you can use as well. These include technical trading, intraday trading, fundamental trading, as well as position trading. Try out as many of these strategies and then identify that works out for you and fits your needs.

Currency Pairs

Now keep in mind that Forex currency is always traded in pairs. What this simply means is that two currencies are paired together and the price of one is quoted in reference to the other. As such, these currency pairs are essential components of currency trade. Also, the prices of the currencies keep changing all the time depending on a number of factors.

Earlier we had mentioned that currencies are classified as the majors, the minor ones, and the exotic currencies. The majors include the currencies of the US, Canada, UK, and European Union. These are among some of the worlds' largest economies. A major is a currency pair that includes the US dollar. Examples include EUR/USD, AUD/USD and JPY/USD. Minors are currency pairs that do not include the US dollar. For instance, JPY/EUR, AUD/NZD and so on are considered minor pairs. Exotic currencies are currencies that do not belong to major world economies. They include the Hong Kong Dollar, Norwegian Kroner, and the Russian Rubble among others.

We also refer to the pricing and quotation structure of currencies as a currency pair. When you choose your preferred currency pairs, you will then proceed to trade these at the Forex markets. You will be simultaneously buying one currency and at the same time selling another. Even then, traders often view currency pairs as a single entity that can be used for trading purposes.

Example

Let us take the example where we have the Euro and US dollar paired together. Hence our currency pair in this instance is the EUR/USD. In this case, we refer to the EUR as the quote currency while the USD is referred to as the base currency. In our case above, the value of the currency pair will simply imply the value of the quote currency needed so as to buy a single unit of the base.

Therefore, the ask price simply refers to the price of selling a particular currency pair while the bid price refers to cost or price of purchasing a currency pair. When you are in the Forex market buying a currency of a particular trade, then you will be said to have taken a long position. In this instance, you will be hoping that the price will rise higher until such a time as when you are ready to sell. You will then sell at an attractive and worthwhile profit.

In some instances, you may need to get to the Forex market to sell your currency pairs. When you do this, you will be entering a short position and hoping to sell your currencies for a tidy profit. You will make a profit in this instance which will be the difference between the price at which you bought currencies and the selling price.

Base currencies versus quoted currencies

As you deal in Forex currencies, you will be purchasing the base currency then selling the quoted currency. The reverse is true when selling a currency pair. In this case you will offer buyers the base currency and in return you will get paid the quoted currency.

Essential Forex Terminology

The Forex market comes with its own unique jargon and terms. In order to understand what is happening at the markets, you should learn the jargon used by other traders and players in the Forex market. Before you begin trading currencies you will have to understand some basic terminology. These terms pertain to the Forex market and will enable you to understand and interpret different calculations and Forex quotes. It is essential to learn some of these terms so that you become an able and capable trader.

- **Cross rate:** This term refers to the exchange rate between two different currencies. In most cases, these currencies are usually not the main currencies of the country where the quotes are issued. The term is sometimes used to refer to currencies that are not paired with the US dollar.

    As an example, consider the situation where a currency pair including the British Pound and the New Zealand dollar is quoted in a Canadian magazine. This currency pair can be referred to as a cross rate. However, if the currency pair involved the US dollar, then it would not be a cross rate.

    Leverage: In Forex trading, the term leverage refers to the provision to control a huge sum of money in the markets. Most Forex trading

Using leverage, you can make pretty attractive returns from your trades especially because of the small and minute movements that regularly occur on the trading platform. You need to be extremely cautious, however, when you use leverage because even though you stand to make astronomical profits, you also stand to lose huge amounts of money.

Exchange rate: This refers to the actual value of a single currency when it is expressed in terms of a different currency. As an example, if we have USD/CAD as 1.2800, this means that 1 USD is equivalent to CAD 1.2800.

Spread: Any quote will have a bid and offer price or the buy and sell quotes. The difference between these prices is what is known as spread. As an example, if we have a USD/CAD quote expressed as 1.2800/02, then the spread in this case is equal to the difference between 1.2800 and 1.2802. This difference is read as 2 pips.

Pips: The term pip is very common when it comes to Forex trade. It simply refers to the difference between the values of two currencies. Therefore, when you have a currency at $1.1200 and another at $1.1250, then the difference between the two is referred to as 50 pips.

Pip actually refers to the last decimal position on a currency pair quotation. They are often used when traders use either two or four decimal places in their quotes. Pips are sometimes referred to as points or a point. In generally, a pip is simply the tiniest increment in the price movement of a currency.

Margin: When you begin trading, you will be required to deposit a certain amount into your trading account by your broker. This is the amount that you will use to trade. It is also the amount where any fees and costs will be charged. Therefore, the deposit that is needed to maintain a position is basically known as the margin.

Margin amount can be either used or free. A free margin is an amount that is required to open a new position in the Forex markets while a used margin is one that is necessary to maintain an already open position. Let us assume that you have about $1000 in your trading account and need 1% in order to open a position in the market. This basically means that you deal in a position that is worth a total of $100,000.

A margin call can be made by a broker when an account drops to levels that are below the amounts needed to hold open positions. Therefore, when your accounts fall below the minimum amount, you can expect a margin call from your broker. In some cases, the broker will close the trade should the amount available be less than that required. Sometimes brokers set the limit which is often about 50% of the amount needed to open a trade.

Hedging: This term refers to a new position being opened by a trader but in the opposite direction. When you open a new position that is directly opposite a current position, you will be said to have taken a hedging position. This is especially when trading the same currency pairs. For instance, if you wish to hedge a 0.2 buy position on the

CAD/NZD, then all you need to do is to open a 0.2 sell position on the same currency pair. When you hedge a position, you will not require additional margin.

Swaps or Rollovers: Sometimes Forex traders get a chance to not just earn profits but also to make capital gains. When we trade currency pairs, we also involve two varying interest rates. Sometimes you will not just make a profit from trading interests but also from an increase in interest rates.

Should the rates increase, then you will earn what is known as a rollover or interest. Sometimes the interest rate may fall. In this case, you will have a negative rollover. When the rollovers are positive, they will add to your profits. However, when they are negative, your trades may incur additional costs.

Commissions: Traders have to pay fees, charges, and commissions to their brokers. The fees and commissions will vary from broker to broker based on certain factors.

Nicknames for most major Forex pairs

Most major currencies traded on the Forex markets have certain nicknames attached to them. These make it easier for traders and others in the sector to easily identify them. Here are some of the common terms used to refer to major currency combinations.

1. EUR/USD – the Euro
2. AUD/USD – Aussie dollar
3. GBP/ USD – Sterling or Cable
4. USD/JPY - Dollar Yen
5. NZD/USD – Kiwi
6. USD/CHF – Swissy
7. USD/CAD – Dollar Canada

How to read Forex quotes

If you intend to trade the Forex markets and make a profit, then you will need to lean how to accurately read currency quotes. This is necessary before you begin trading. As we have already seen previously, currencies are paired together in Forex.

You will notice that foreign currencies are often quoted in pairs. This is because we are expressing the value of one currency using the other. You can also view this is as selling one currency while simultaneously buying another. Let us look at an example of a quote.

USD/AUD = 1.2800

The USD component in the above quote is referred to as the base currency while the AUD component is referred to as the quote currency. The quote currency is also known as the counter.

When you purchase a currency pair, then the quoted exchange rate will reveal the amount of the quoted currency needed to purchase the base currency. For instance, in the above the example, you will need to pay 1.2800 Australian dollars to purchase 1 US dollar. On the other hand, if you were to sell one US dollar, you will receive 1.2800 Australian dollars.

The Bid and Ask Prices

Ask price – the ask price is basically at which you buy a particular currency pair. It is the price at which your broker or the market is willing to sell you a specific currency pair. The ask price basically allows you to purchase a single unit of your base currency.

Bid price – this is the price at which you will sell your currency pair. It is also the price at which the market, or your broker, is willing to purchase currencies from you. The bid price is the price at which you will sell a single unit of the base currency.

Bid/Ask spread: The bid/ask spread is simply the difference between ask and the bid prices. Spreads often varies from one broker to another.

Chapter 3: Forex Trading Strategies

Now that you have learned the basics of Forex trading, it is time now to delve deeper and learn about actual trading strategies. Trading strategies can be termed as techniques used by traders to enable them decide whether to sell or buy a currency pair at a specific time.

Fundamental and Technical Analysis

When applying Forex trading strategies, we use outcomes of either fundamental analysis or technical analysis. Therefore, before you start trading, you mush conduct some analysis so as to know the best currency pairs to sell or buy and the most appropriate time to do so. Apart from the outcome of the analysis, a strategy should also include trading signals.

However, you do not always have to conduct the analysis yourself if you do not want to even though it is highly recommended. There are experts who do this on behalf of others and provide outcomes online. You can find analysis on the internet which you can then use for your trading strategy.

Discipline

One of the most important aspects of a good trading strategy is that it should first and foremost be well thought out and back-tested. This means that the strategy should be proven to work well even after implementation. As such, you should implement the strategy once you are ready and then stick with it. You should not change your mind mid-way but stick with a strategy to the end.

As a trader, you will require self-discipline. This is the only route to success. All too often, young or novice traders enter a trade by implementing a strategy then begin to panic shortly thereafter. When you let emotions lead you, then you will never make any profits and will lose money. This is because emotions will lead you to think that you are losing money. Instead, be disciplined and stick to a strategy. Let the strategy run its course just as long as you implement it correctly and follow it as required.

Putting together a strategy

Trading strategies for Forex traders can be automated or manual. These are used to generate trading signals. Manual systems require that you sit on a computer and find the signals then determine whether or not you should buy. On the other hand we have automated systems. These require the trader to develop a suitable algorithm that identifies trade signals and then executes them all on its own. This is a preferred approach basically because it eliminates the emotion out of the trade. This way, you get to improve your performance. It is advisable to take caution when buying strategies from different places online. This is because it is rather difficult to track down the performance of these strategies. A lot of successful trading systems are never revealed to the public. You will also need to make a determination about the currency pairs you wish to trade. Once you do, you should then work to become an expert at studying the specific currency pair.

Most of the times when traders speak of Forex strategies they usually refer to particular methods that can be applied to trades. However, these often are just an aspect of a total plan. A strategy will mostly point you towards a favorable entry point. This is the best point at which you should enter the market. However, apart from these, you should also consider other aspects. These include the following;

- Most favorable entry points
- Position sizing
- Best exit points
- Risk management techniques
- Trading tactics

There are a number of trading strategies out there so choosing the best and most profitable is crucial. A good strategy can be one that appeals to you as an individual. It should be one that you are comfortable and happy with. Only if this is the case will you thrive and become profitable. If you try some other strategy simply because it worked for someone else, then this will probably not work out. Basically what works out for someone else may not necessarily work out for you. This is why you need to practice a lot and try out as many different strategies as possible. Only then will you find out the strategy that best matches your personality.

On the other hand, it is very possible as well, that a strategy that worked out for someone else also works out for you. At this stage, the key is as much practice on demo platforms as possible and learning self-disciplined. If you learn from the onset to be a disciplined trader then you will definitely be on your way to success. A disciplined trader is one who spends time identifying a suitable strategy then sticks with their strategy to the end.

As a trader, you should set up a trading system on platforms such as Meta Trader. On this platform, you are able to automate your trading instructions. This way, you will first come up with a strategy, develop the appropriate execution technologies. When you automate a trade and put a stop loss measure as well as take profit point, you should comfortably let the trade take its course. When you use a platform such as Meta Trader, you will also be able to perform a back test just to confirm how your strategy will play out in the real market.

Trading styles

There are a number of very popular trading styles adapted by traders around the world. These strategies range from short to long-time frames. They have been successfully implemented over the years and are still popular even today. As a Forex trader, you need to be aware of the various strategies and styles for successful trading. This way, you can always navigate from one trading style to another should you feel that there is one not particularly working for you.

1. Day trading: When you execute day trading strategy, you will have to exit a trade before the close of the day. This means that you enter a trade in the morning or sometime during the day and exit before the day ends. As a beginner, this strategy can be one of the best because it saves you from any shocks or losses that may occur during the night. Day trades usually last only a couple of hours. This way, you are able to enter a trade after doing your analysis, rake in some profits, and then exit when you can. A suitable example of day trading strategy is the 50-pips.

2. Scalping: Scalping is a trading strategy that lasts a very short period of time. You simply enter a position on the Forex markets and shortly thereafter you exit and collect your profits. The aim of this strategy is to try and beat the bid-offer spread and then make a modest profit before exiting the trade. Scalping makes use of tick charts so you know exactly when to enter and at what point you should exit a trade. You should also ensure that you make use of scalping indicators provide via tools which are readily available to you.

3. Position trading: This is a strategy where a trader follows the trend. It is a long term strategy with the aim of maximizing profitability especially in instances where there are huge price movements. When you adapt this approach, you will mostly be inspecting end-of-day charts. You will also need to be a rather patient investor with a deep understanding of market fundamentals.

4. *Swing trading:* A trader using this approach will basically hold a position for a couple of days. This time period is often between a single day and an entire week even though this period can sometimes extend into weeks and months. As a swing trader, you will typically inspect charts in thirty-minute intervals.

Additional Forex Trading Strategies

50 Pips per Day

This is a Forex trading strategy that seeks to benefit from early market movement especially of very liquid currencies. The most liquid currencies are the USD, GBP, and the EUR. These are the best to deal in and the most ideal especially for this particular strategy.

Often on early mornings, different Forex traders place dual positions and sometimes two pending orders. As soon as one of these positions is activated through price movement, the other position gets cancelled immediately.

This strategy targets a profit of 50 pips and has a stop-loss order ranging between 6 and 10 pips. This stop-loss order is often placed below or above the 07.00 candlestick GMT time. Stop-loss orders are placed to prevent losses. When your position in the market starts to lose money, it will only do so to a pre-determined point before automatically exiting. Exiting a position at a predetermined point helps prevent further losses. Risk management is essential in this case because this approach is highly risky.

Daily charts strategy

A lot of experienced Forex traders prefer trading the daily charts instead of other strategies such as the short-term ones. Daily charts have less market noise compared to others such as the Forex 1-hour charts and others with lower timeframes. Using the daily charts can enable you gain over 100 pips each day since they come with longer timeframes.

Also, daily charts provide signals that are a lot more reliable compared to other signals and chances of earning a huge profit are much better. There is also no need for fundamental analysis or worries regarding random price changes or daily news. There are however 3 main factors that affect this trade.

1. Identify the trend: You first need to identify the trend. This is crucial because markets first trend and then consolidate. This is a process that repeats over and over so be on the lookout for the trend.

A reliable way of locating the trend is to study prior Forex data for approximately 180 periods. This data will enable you identify upswings and downswings as well. When you do this, you will easily be able to identify the trend.

2. Remain focused: As a trader, you need to be patient and allow trades to take their course. You need to be able to manage the urge of exiting trades prematurely. This calls for discipline and focus. Stay focused on current trade and trust that your analysis is correct.

3. Make use of large stop losses and less leverage: You need to be on the lookout for the occasional intraday swings which can sometimes be quite large. The best approach to mitigate these large swings is to use stops that are sufficiently large.

Trend-following Strategies

Markets always set a trend then follow this trend for a considerable time. However, sometimes the trend tends to experience sharp price spikes which could head up or down. This is often as a result of volatility. In other situations, the market may move outside the range. It may then trend above the line of resistance or below the support line so that a new trend actually starts. When the trend moves below the support line, then traders begin to keep off. The reason is that more and more low prices get established. This means opportunities are being created to allow them to enter trades at much cheaper prices. Traders often wait until the trend bottoms out. At the same time there could be traders who begin to panic and sell their currencies as fast as possible.

However, the trend continues until the price settles down without the risk of further downward spiral. Buying when the currency prices are down and selling at higher price is the aim of Forex traders.

This way you will be able to make a tidy profit in the end. Traders often feel encouraged to purchase currency pairs in the open market once the trend breaks through the resistance.

In some instances trends tend to be prolonged and even dramatic. Since there is plenty of movement in the markets, the trend is often thought of as the best Forex strategy especially for beginners. Forex trading systems that follow the market trend use indicators that alert traders whenever new trends set in even though there is no sure way of determining this.

Positive outlook

Now when signal indicators point to a specific time when a trend started, then the odds will swing in your favor. A breakout is the instance where we notice a trend that is just about to begin. Systems that follow the trend need traders with a specific mindset because you can lose profits should the markets experience a sudden swing. As such you really need to be mentally strong and psychologically prepared for such an eventuality.

The 4-Hour Trading Strategy

There is yet another profitable and beneficial strategy that you can consider using. This is the 4-hour trend strategy which is more suitable for the swing trader. Traders use the 4-hour charts to find signals that indicate the best market entry points. You also need to use the 1-hour charts in order to determine or confirm the exact position to assume in the Forex market.

Counter – Trend Strategy

We also have the counter-trend strategy. This is a strategy that counts on the fact that any breakout trends never end up as long-term trends but will fizzle out eventually. It is crucial to observe that this approach does require strict risk management. There is a good reason for this. For instance, the strategy basically relies on resistance and support levels remaining firm. Should they fail and instances such as large downsides occur, then potential losses will be significant.

As a trader, you will need to monitor the markets constantly. This regular monitoring will help to keep your account safe. For the best outcome, you will need to be in a volatile yet stable market. Such an environment is crucial as it offers attractive price swings which are managed within a range.

You need to be aware that the status of a market can change without much warning. An otherwise quiet and stable market can begin to trend then experience volatility before calm returns. These changes are often unpredictable and uncertain. Therefore always examine the state of the market before choosing to enter.

Technical indicators

There are certain things that will assist with your strategy. These are technical indicators. A lot of these indicators have been developed in the recent past. They provide crucial information that you need as a trader if you are to execute trades successfully.

In all, the best and most preferred Forex strategies are those that are well-established, simple, and easy to understand. These strategies have worked for numerous traders over the years and have helped produce some of the best traders in the market today. You need to a lot of practice using demo accounts and try trading using different strategies. It is only through such practice that you will be able to determine which specific strategy works best for you.

Best Indicators for Forex Trading

When you begin trading Forex, you will be successful if you follow the path that many others have in the past. You first need to know how to trade. This is crucial. To trade successfully, you will need to make use of trade indicators and specifically technical indicators for the Forex market.

Technical Indicators

Technical indicators are simply tools of a mathematical nature that you use to analyze factors pertaining to Forex trading. These factors are open and closing prices, volumes, high and low. The indicators, once calculated, are plotted on graphs which can then be read and interpreted. These graphs are referred to as chart patterns. To be a successful trader, you will need to learn how to read charts.

Most of the current technical indicators were actually designed for daily charts and the stock market. The reason is because back then charts were only updated for a maximum 24-hour period. This was many years before the internet was created. There are different types of indicators that you can use. These include the following;

- Trend indicators
- Volume indicators
- Momentum indicators
- Volatility indicators

Changing a Forex Trading Strategy

Basically when you implement a strategy it should work out well for you. However, a strategy is only effective if you follow all the rules. Most traders find this to be true whenever they implement a strategy. In rare cases though some strategies simply do not work and they may need to be changed.

A strategy that is effective today may not necessarily be a successful strategy tomorrow. In short, any strategy that does not make you money, is not producing results and is not profitable can be changed. But before changing your strategy you should consider the following measures.

1. Try and match trading style with risk management: Examine the risk versus reward ratio and determine if it is working. If it is unsuitable at this point, then you may want to change the strategy and adapt one that actually works for you.

2. Understanding a strategy: Sometimes traders really do not grasp a strategy. Failure to fully comprehend a strategy may lead to failure and the strategy basically wont work. This calls for changing strategy to one that the trader comprehends.

3. Changing market conditions: Some strategies depend on certain market conditions. If you implement a strategy that heavily relies on conditions in the market, then changing conditions may affect the strategy. In this case, you may need to adjust you strategy and find one that works for the prevailing market conditions.

While a change of strategy is recommended in some instances, it can sometimes prove to be costly. Try not to modify your strategies too often and instead trust your analysis and back-testing. If not then you stand to lose out immensely. Here are some key points to note.

- A Forex strategy is simply a trading technique used for trading currencies and generating profits in the Forex market

- You will often need to use certain tools to support and guide your trading strategy. These tools are often digital even though there are manual ones
- Before implementing any strategy, you should first back-test it and then implement it on a demo platform. Allow it to run before eventually implementing it live on the markets.

As an example, a novice trader first determines that the USD/JPY is a currency with plenty of potential and he foresees it doing well in the near future. Before trading though he performs his technical analysis. Using one of the moving averages he determines a trend in the market. The trader then goes ahead to trade the USD/JPY currency pair and make some attractive returns in the process.

Essential Things to Make you a Successful Forex Trader

As it is, there is not one single strategy of formula for success trading the Forex market. A great way to view Forex trading is to view the markets as the ocean and traders are the surfers. Surfing is a sport that requires skills. The more you practice the more your skill improves. Also, to be a great surfer, you need certain tools such as proper surfing board, swimming kit, and so on. Other essentials include proper balance, talent, discipline, and being comfortable in the deep sea.

If you had a great fear of deep waters or lacked proper balance then you would not make a great surfer. The same is true when it comes to Forex trading. You need to have all the essential ingredients if you are to succeed and be profitable. If you do not have the necessary tools and skills then you should not enter the water and surf the waves. Similarly, avoid the Forex market until you learn how to trade and become profitable.

To become a successful trader you need to have proper analytical skills, the necessary tools, and proper implementation techniques. All these essential skills and techniques are summarized below.

1. Your approach to Forex

One of the most important things you need to do before you begin trading is to prepare as much as possible. Proper preparation is key to successful Forex trading. Think about your personal aims and your temperament and persona. If you really understand Forex, then you will do better in that market. however, if you feel inclined towards something else such as stocks or futures, then pause and think things over.

2. Time frame

When you want to start trading, think about the timeframes involved. This is because there are different strategies and most vary with time. There are 5-minute charts, day trading, swing trading, and so on. Are you comfortable holding overnight positions? You should also consider incurring losses on days when trades do not work in your favor.

Think about your lifestyle. Are you busy and wish to trade Forex in your spare time? Then think about trading evenings only. Also, are you intending to start trading as a full time occupation? Then there are strategies that allow you to do this. Think about day trading for instance. You can enter the markets, watch your screen all day and exit at day's end. It's crucial though to keep in mind that you can make huge profits trading the Forex markets but success comes with time and not overnight.

3. Trading attitude

Your trading attitude is closely related to your behavior. As such, your behavior will have a huge impact on certain characteristics. These include discipline, patience, realistic expectations and objectivity. Discipline is the choice and ability to be patient and let a trade run its course.

There will be occasion when the price action will not get to your expected price level. When this happens, your first instinct would be to pull away from the markets to avoid losses. However, this is not a smart approach and you should stick to your plan. Trust the systems in place to work in your favor. However, should your stop loss management system ask you to pull out of the market then you should do so without hesitating.

Objectivity here refers to emotional detachment. You need to be able to eliminate all forms of emotion from your trades. Emotional trade is a weakness that many novices exhibit. They notice the first sign of losses and choose to exit for fear of losing their money.

4. Implementing a Forex strategy

Experts have already demonstrated that there is absolutely nothing like a profitable trade only. This is because even the best and most seasoned Forex traders lose money. Profitability is found in proper execution of trades and risk management techniques used.

Eventually, everything will boil down to your risk management and control. To achieve risk management successfully, you will need to ensure that your strategy starts of in the correct direction. Keep watching the performance of your trade and the system in place. Should any adjustments be necessary then make them as early as possible. You will probably get your direction right after the second or third attempt.

In summary

In conclusion, we can conclude that Forex trading is as much an art as it a science. This means you need multiple skills as well as proper state of mind to succeed. You will either make or lose money depending on how you apply your techniques and according to your discipline. You can always take small losses as these are part of being a trader. Take these quickly so as to avoid the larger more devastating loss.

Chapter 4: Best Trade Entry and Exit Strategies

Trade entries are a huge determinant of whether your trades will be successful or not. Most traders tend to take entry points for granted and focus their energies on the actual trade. A shift from this approach towards application of the best trade entry strategies will significantly improve the risk-reward potential of any trade and also helps you to achieve a superior stop loss location.

As a trader, one of the most essential aspects you need to focus on is establishing if there is a trend in the market or not. Ordinarily, you would simply need to trade with the trend setup or consider setting up a countertrend reversal setup.

It is crucial that you learn how to determine the best Forex entry methods and the essential tools you require for market entry. There are a couple of different methods that you can use to successfully enter the market. If practiced consistently, they will enable you become a more proficient trader.

1. Assess the Market

As a Forex trader, you need to recognize the environment in which the market is operating. By identifying the operating environment, you will then be able to establish the most appropriate strategies and tactics at any given time. You need to determine what kind of market structure you would like to trade and what type of trades you wish to make.

2. Scan your Charts

Among the first things you need to do before the start of your trading day is to scan your charts. You should first determine the best Forex pairs to trade then scan the charts. One of the best approaches is to scan the markets right after the closure of New York and the opening of European markets. During these hours, the market action goes down after the previous trading day.

Even as you scan the charts, be on the lookout for price action, levels, and trends. It is important to look out for a trend. For instance, watch out for any patterns that involve low highs and low lows or higher highs and higher lows. Also be on the lookout for the direction of the 21 and 8 daily EMAs.

3. Establish a Trend

You should endeavor to establish a trend. It all comes down to looking for the higher highs and higher lows versus the lower lows and lower highs. If you can establish a crystal clear trend, then it will be worth much more than gold. Successful traders always trade along a trend and rarely against it.

4. Try and Set Up Trades at the End of Each Day

This is a very easy yet very effective approach. If you can set up your trade at the close of New York markets, then you will have an effective start. You will also eliminate any mental confusion and noise brought on by use of intraday charts. You should ensure that you monitor all your trades once or twice each trading day in order not to unnecessarily fiddle with the trades. This will also help to eliminate the psychological aspect of trading.

As a trader, you either specialize in one type of trading or are a master in several types and can choose a preferred type depending on market situation. It is important to keep this in mind when building your strategy. For a trader who has mastered different trading styles, the best approach is to focus on only a few currencies while a specialized trader should focus on scanning the market and viewing more Forex currency pairs.

Scanning the Market

When scanning the markets, the aim is to look for the following;

- Price action
- Trends
- Levels

What you need to determine first is whether there is a trend in the market. This is ideally not a science but actually an art. Patterns of high highs and low lows are crucial at this stage because they point to a trend.

Get Better Prices with Limiting Orders

A limiting order is also known as a pending order. It is placed above or below the prevailing market price depending on the direction of the trade. Limiting orders provide you with the ability to enter a trade at a price of your choosing. The only challenge is that you may not always get into a trade at all.

If you are trading short, the limiting order should be set just above the prevailing market price. However, if you are trading long, then the limiting order should be placed below the prevailing market price. Here is how to apply the limiting order.

1. The Trade Entry Tip: This is where a trader enters a price action signal on a 50% retrace. It simply means that you enter a limited order where the price retraces back to the 50% level of a pin bar. This approach greatly improves your risk vs. reward ratio and it allows you to place a tighter stop loss. You will easily be able to double your returns.

Another benefit of this approach is that you have more flexibility regarding where you place or locate your stop loss. You can choose the normal distance stop loss or enter a trade with a much tighter stop loss. You get more breathing space within your trades as a trader when you use a regular stop loss distance using a limit entry order on a pin bar. Limit orders enable you to attract the market your way because you only enter a trade if it moves towards your preferred price. There are chances of missing out on the trade simply because the price may not necessary reach your preferred level. However, it is much better to use this approach because of the flexibility it offers.

2. Daily chart time frame: This chart time frame is a lot more relevant in setting out your entry points than you may be aware. This is because it is more useful than other charts with low time frames. The daily chart can be considered to be a natural filter for any bad entries. It actually filters out irrelevant and outstanding price movement of the lower time frame. Because of this, the daily chart signals become a lot more reliable.

Essential Tools for Market Entry

1. For the level pickers

Fibonacci retracement, trendline bounce, chart pattern bounce, bottom and top of range, the highs and lows, the top and bottom, and the Fibonacci target.

2. For the momentum breakout traders

Chart pattern breaks, break of the bottom or top, the trend line breaks, a fractal indicator break, and a break of the low or high.

3. For confirmation traders

Tools such as indicator confirmations, fractal break in anticipated direction, and candlestick formations in regions where support and resistance are expected.

Trade Style and Psychology

Generally, traders will have a preference of an entry strategy. This preference will depend on the trading psychology and style. There are traders who prefer to wait for a momentum break and cannot handle early entries. Others prefer to trade a pullback as these enable them to plan early. The trading psychology and style are crucial factors that often influence the entry strategy.

Stop Loss Strategies

It is almost impossible for any trader to survive the Forex markets without a reasonable risk management strategy. A stop loss strategy is one of the most important risk management strategies available to traders. Learning about the crucial stop loss strategies is absolutely essential.

The good news is that with stop loss orders, you will easily be able to protect your trades from negative emotions like fear and greed. If unchecked, such emotions can cause havoc to your trades.

What is a Stop Loss Order?

A stop loss order is simply any order that you place so that a security that you hold is sold when a certain price is achieved. The order is usually placed with your Forex broker. Such an order is created in order to minimize the losses a trader might incur after taking a position. It is absolutely imperative to institute stop loss orders any time a trade is initiated.

There are a couple of ways that such an order can be implemented. This is why it is important to actually come up with a good strategy that will suit a particular trade, market, or situation.

1. The Initial Stop Loss Placement

This particular stop loss strategy largely depends on the trading strategy that you choose. While there are some personal preferences that can come into play, it is one that is definitely common with many Forex traders.

If you adopt the pin bar trading strategy, then the stop loss can be placed directly behind the tail end of the pin bar. This move applied to both the bearish and bullish pin bars.

With the inside bar trading strategy, you should place the stop loss either behind the inside bar's low or high, or behind the mother bar's low or high. In both these cases, should the price hit the stop loss, they strategies become invalid and this simply means the set up was not sufficiently strong.

2. The Hands Off Stop Loss Strategy

Another excellent stop loss option that you can apply is the "Set and Forget" strategy which is also known as the "Hands Off" strategy. The aim of this strategy is very simple. As a trader simply set your stop loss strategy and just let the market run its course. It alleviates any chance of getting stopped way too soon as the stop loss is maintained at a relatively safe distance.

This strategy doesn't involve your hands so that you do not have to do anything once it is set up. The aim here is to ensure there is no temptation to make adjustments on the stop loss as you trade. There are some obvious advantages of using this particular method. These are listed below.

- Keeps emotional trading under control
- Eliminates the chance of getting stopped too early

- Frees up the trader so they focus on trades
- It is a very simple policy to implement

This kind of approach helps to reduce chances that a trade will be stopped too early by ensuring the stop loss is placed at a far enough distance. As traders, we know the challenges of moving the stop loss too early as our trades are stopped only to see the markets proceed in the correct direction.

It is imperative that emotions are eliminated from your trades. This way, reason will prevail and you will be successful in your trades thanks to this stop loss measure. All you do once you set up the stop loss is to simply sit back and let the market take its course. Also, this stop loss method is simple to implement because it is only handled once. Then as soon as it is set up, you can forget about it.

However, there are some disadvantages or downside of this particular set up measure. These are recounted below.

- Traders are often tempted to move the stop loss closer to entry point
- High risk because traders stand to lose the maximum possible amount

A trader who puts $500 on a trade stands to lose this amount as it is also the maximum possible amount that can be lost. This is risky and should therefore be approached with caution.

Sometimes traders feel the temptation to move the stop loss from where it is to where they feel safer. The Forex market is wrought with temptations and a disciplined trader should learn to fend off such temptations.

3. Break Even Stop Loss Measure

Yet another useful and applicable stop loss measure that we can institute is the break even strategy. Lessons on stop loss strategies are incomplete without this particular method. Traders often adopt this measure in order to protect their capital. Traders feel safe that they cannot lose money using this stop loss strategy.

Often, you will find traders moving their stop loss close to the entry price. This is not a bad strategy but at least it protects you as a trader. Here are some of the benefits of this strategy.

- You do not need to conduct market analysis with this strategy
- It is a very simple strategy to implement
- It gets rid of any imminent risk of a given trade

Once this strategy is in place, any risk to the trade is eliminated. Any market movements will then be protected by your stop loss measure, keeping you safe as the market plays out. Also, you will not need to conduct any complex, or simple, market analysis. Simply determine your entry point and use it to determine your stop loss.

The break even stop loss strategy is also one of the easiest strategies to implement. It is always easy to know where to place the stop loss no matter the trade. Even then, this measure has some disadvantages.

- This strategy hinders your odds
- It makes use of an arbitrary level which is not the best approach
- It puts traders at risk of emotional trading

Because the only determinant of the stop loss measure depends on your entry point and not market analysis, then this is an arbitrary approach. Such an approach does not portend much success compared to others.

This strategy will limit most likely limit your chances of success because it does not give any of your trades a chance to be successful. There is not enough room to move and maneuver. This is in contrast to the price action confluence that should essentially give you better odds. However, this stop loss strategy does allow the price action confluence to be in your favor and therefore affects your odds.

4. The 50% Stop Loss Strategy

This is a strategy that aims at cutting your risks by 50%. However, it does not necessarily cut your risks by exactly half. The main benefit of applying this strategy is that it makes use of the markets and enables traders to understand how much of their capital they need to protect.

Basically, if you apply this strategy and enter the market based on the daily close, the market may close slightly higher the following day. Now you can choose the day's low to determine your stop loss measure. Now, when the markets close the following day after your entry, you can use the low of that day to determine the stop loss point. This way, you will cut your risk by half. What this simply states is that should the market go below the previous day's low, then you will not proceed with the trade. There are some outright advantages of this kind of set up.

- Allows the use of the price action level
- Will cut your risk by up to 50%
- Gives your trades sufficient room to breathe

Cutting your risk by half is beneficial and actually good for your trades. For instance, if one of your trades was worth $100, then you could easily ensure that you lose no more than 50% on this trade.

This strategy makes use of the price action level. Due to this, it is unlikely that the market will get to the stop loss. In this instance, the market lows and highs are in play and hence the stop is protected. This is a much better approach as compared to other strategies such as the break even stop loss strategy.

Also this system allows the market space to breath. This means trades can freely occur without a trader having to exit. Market movements are essential if you are to make money trading Forex currencies. However, there are some downsides to this strategy. For instance;

- There is still the possibility of stopping trades prematurely
- Trades are still at 50% risk of loss

Although this strategy allows your trades to get some much needed breathing space, the trades are at risk of being stopped prematurely. This fact is particularly true for trades that involve currency pairs with volatile price action. Also, your trades will be at a 50% risk of losing out. This can be acceptable for some trades but unacceptable to others.

You can use market conditions during trade to determine whether the 50% stop loss strategy is the most suitable for your purpose. Take for example a situation where the market closed very close to the previous day's low. Then in such a situation, the 50% strategy would not work because it would have to be too close to the prevailing market rates.

Monitor your Stop Loss

When the market starts to move in a direction that favors you, then you should consider trailing your stop loss. Trailing the stop loss when the market is trending in your direction will help you protect your trading capital. It is important to note that a stop loss can be monitored either automatically or manually. Most modern trading platforms offer traders this option so they can choose if they wish to trail the stop loss or not.

The automated one is generally managed by the system so you will not necessarily need to worry about it. However, when manually following it, you will need to use price action levels in order to determine the trailing point of the stop loss.

Example

Take for example a trade situation where you purchase the Euro USD at 1.35. You can set the trailing stop loss at approximately 50 pips. Assume that the market actually moves in your favor and you gain up to 1.39 and this move gains you 400 pips. The stop loss will now adjust to 1.355.

It is therefore essential that you trail the stop loss marker manually, whenever possible, using indicators such as the price action levels. This way, you will remain safe and will use reliable indicators that give you more room to maneuver and allow trades to prosper.

It is absolutely critical that you use stop loss strategies as a Forex trader. There are a couple of strategies available so you will need to determine which is the most appropriate for each trade. For this, you will need to master how to use confluence to your advantage, how to use the best risk-reward ratio and how to define price action strategies and determining key levels.

Importance of Setting a Small Short Order

You need to set small short orders for a number of reasons. For starters, such short orders help to protect you from losses. This is essentially why it is so named. You trade to make money and not lose it. A small short order achieves this effectively.

The first and most important benefit of using a small short order is that it limits the losses to within acceptable margins. This is important because it protects your capital and limits exposure.

You can also effectively use it to lock in profits. This is why a short order is sometimes referred to as a trailing order. Locking in profits is crucial for Forex traders because profit is the main reason why we trade.

The short stop loss order also helps eliminate emotion from a trade. When feelings get involved and a trader uses emotions, then his trade will most likely fail and he will lose money.

There are some traders who do not use stop loss measures and instead allow a losing trade to run hoping the market will run and turn the trade around. This is a wrong approach that could cost you money and affect your trading capital. You should instead use a stop loss placement to mitigate losses.

Profit Taking Strategies

Every trader enters the Forex market in order to trade and realize a profit. All traders in the Forex markets have their own trading strategies. However, at the end of the trading day, they need to make money. It can be disastrous for a trader to spend precious hours trading the markets only to see their profits disappear simply because they did not know when and where to exit. Being able to identify the most appropriate exit points is crucial for successful trading on the Forex markets.

Even the best or most experienced traders need to have effective profit taking strategies otherwise they will lose money and become ineffective traders. Therefore, as a trader, once you are in a trade, your work is not yet done. Rather, it has only just begun. Trade management and exit plans need to be implemented and not overlooked. They are a huge part of trading but, sadly, are often overlooked by many traders. Most of the time the aim is to get out close to the top but actually the main objective is to make money. Here is a look at some of the most popular take profit strategies used by successful Forex traders.

Importance of Trade Exits

According to experts, trade management and exits are the most crucial factors of any Forex trade. They are even more important that the entry strategies. However, and surprisingly, not many traders pay attention to the management and exit strategies. Yet exits have the capacity to make or break a trade strategy.

According to research by trade experts and writers, no two traders approach trades the same way even under similar conditions. In most cases, the trader with the best trade management and exit skills will emerge the winner. Those without proper exit strategies may even incur losses.

Trade performance depends on a couple of factors that including trade management, limiting losses, and profit taking techniques. However, applying these techniques is not as easy as it sounds and many traders often fair poorly in this regard.

There are plenty of reasons why many trades are not profitable. Here is a look at some of these reasons.

- Watching a price move only to see it reverse direction before taking profits
- Exiting a position at an average price due to price retracement
- Traders sometimes move a stop loss and they opt to break even too soon

- Placing the take profit position close to the open price halfway in a trade
- Closing a trade too early and denying the take profit position to be attained
- Missing a market reversal and then losing all profits accrued

As traders, our instincts are always to grab a profit whenever the chance presents itself. This is natural and very common as we avoid losing the profit. However, this is never advisable. It is important to resist the temptation of taking profits early and learn to let the trade run its course. Delayed gratification in this case is way more profitable compared to instant gratification.

As a Forex trader, you really should learn patience and practice it as you trade. Also, you need to learn to stick to your original plan. All too often, traders change their minds and divert from the original plan. You will get much better results if you stick with the trade and initial plan.

1. Ensure that you Ride Winners Adequately

There is a saying about assurances in any trade. Basically, there are only two certainties that can occur. As a trader you will have winning trades and you will also have losing trades. To be a successful trader, you will have to learn to ride the winning trades adequately.

To be a successful trader, you should ensure that you fund your ongoing successful trades in order to make even larger profits. Let us assume that, as a trader, you have done your due diligence such as use technical analysis. If this analysis indicates that a winning trade still has some way to go, then you can pump in more funds into this trade so that you earn a much bigger profit.

Many professional traders say often that the success of their trades lies largely in riding on winning trades. There are a couple of ways to ride on a winning trade. One of the most popular ways of doing this is apply the pyramid process. This process simply means pouring in more money onto the winning trade with the hope of maximizing profits. Here is how the approach works.

- Let us assume the initial trade is allocated$15000
- The risk on this trade is put at $300

- A second position is then added as soon as the first gets to breakeven
- This second position should mirror the first one so add $15000
- This second trade rises and nears resistance
- You can have another pyramid at 60% so add $9000
- As soon as the resistance point is attained, take profit and exit

You will notice that you earn a lot more profit with this approach compared to letting it proceed to profit level. This is therefore an extremely useful tip that you can apply to earn significantly more money.

As you trade, there are some important aspects that you need to focus on. For instance, try and ensure that your stop loss' initial position is either at breakeven point or better. Ensure that the system where you are trading essentially has the potential to get the solid trending moves. But there is no need of using this approach if the risk-reward ratio is about 1:1.

2. Make Large Profits with Minimal Losses

The adage among traders is to let a winning run continue but exit any losing trades. However, applying this adage is not that easy for traders. This is because when faced with large profits, the instinct is often to lock them in. however, this is not the ideal approach of this particular strategy.

This strategy basically insinuates holding onto a winning position and hanging in there so the profits keep rising. Patience is a requirement for the success of this strategy. Anytime that a trade is heading your way and performing as well or better than expected, then profits will be on the rise. At such a time, you should not be packing and exiting the trade but rather hang in there, hold your nerve, and ensure you profit from the run as much as possible.

Like earlier pointed out, some of the wealthiest and most successful Forex traders are those who capitalized on profitable runs. A lot of the time, traders also need to learn to run away from losing trades. It is said that the first cut is the cheapest which loosely means that exiting a losing trade is beneficial if done quickly. The sooner you exit a losing trader the less money you lose. This will prevent you from suffering larger and more painful losses.

3. You can take your Money and Start Afresh

As a trader, you still have the option of exiting a trade and starting all over again. This strategy is more applicable to short-term active traders such as day traders. The main aim here is to collect sufficient profits from a successful trade within a certain period. Such a strategy does make sense especially to traders who wish to avoid taking risks with overnight trades.

Situations do change occasionally and overnight movements can wipe out any accrued profits. Taking profits within a trade and then closing the position and exiting the trade gives you a chance to start all over again and repeat the process. A lot of active day traders actively pursue this strategy.

There are ideally only two different ways of taking advantage of this profit taking Forex strategy. One is to apply a dollar or percentage profit target. Therefore, you can work out a suitable percentage for any given trade where you will take profits. As soon as the set percentage or dollar amount is attained, you should exit the trade and possibly start a new one. For instance, if you have a dollar amount target of about $500, you will trade until the amount is attained. Once attained, you should exit and then plan on the next trade.

Some traders use technical analysis to determine or guide their trades. Such traders often opt for technical profit levels. They often work with indicators such as the Fibonacci levels, support and resistance levels and so on. It is a great idea to consider using technical levels or indicators that can easily be used on any MT4 chart. This way, you will have an easy and clear indication about when to exit or stay in a trade.

Chapter 5: Top Options Trading Tools

Forex trader need access to a lot more information than what is generally provided through price charts. There are numerous tools they can use in order to trade prudently. The tools used are often referred to as technical analysis tools. These provide a lot of useful information that is essential for successful trading. The additional insights provided provide the necessary ingredients for success.

Technical tools are used in conjunction with chart overlays and statics. This will ensure Forex traders are able to make informed decisions as they trade. Some tools are suitable only for Forex trade while others are suitable for additional use like stock trading.

Trading platforms have what is known as a session highlighter. This feature is programmed to automatically display vertical lines across the price charts anytime that a major trading session closes or opens. Different trading sessions can easily be visually highlighted by the trader using a variety of colors.

Why Traders need Forex Trading Tools

Tools are absolutely indispensable when it comes to Forex trading. Fortunately most of these have become standard and numerous so brokers are able to provide their clients or traders on their platform some of the best tools in the market. A good example of a suitable trading tool is Meta Trader. Here are a couple of useful tools that you can use as you focus on your technique.

1. The Forex Calendar

You are likely to come across the Forex Calendar across different platform. Many brokers and traders provide this calendar on their platforms. Therefore, as a trader, you will most likely encounter this calendar when you enter the market. The Forex calendar contains a lot of information including economic news releases, fundamental events, and all current and previous values. Once information is released, the calendar is then updated so that the new information is also shared with traders.

One of the most common regular events displayed on the Forex calendar is the NFP or the non-farm payroll. The value of this figure changes on a monthly basis. This is why a lot of traders use this calendar as their primary tool when trading during such events.

2. Trading Terminal

Different Forex traders sometimes require different types of trading tools. For instance, if you are a trader observing multiple assets at the same time or a scalper, then the trading terminal is suitable for you. The trading terminal Forex tool enables you to buy and sell multiple currency pairs via the same window. As you trade multiple currencies, you will also be able to manage your trades and establish stop-losses as well as take profits whenever you have to. The terminal is great for multiple other things including numerous other Forex trading tools.

3. Mini terminal

This is a tool that is available with the trading terminal. Therefore, if you are keen on the latter then you should be able to handle the mini terminal. This is a pretty handy tool to have for any Forex trader because it supports Meta Trader's 1 click manager. Using this tool you will be able to do a lot all at once such as set your take-profit and stop-loss points with a single click. You can also purchase and sell Forex with one simple click of your mouse. This is a fantastic tool for most traders and especially day traders like scalpers and others.

4. MS Excel Forex Trader

Microsoft has developed Ms Excel Forex Trader which is an excellent option for Forex traders. A lot of experts in the field of finance use Excel for different applications and it serves them extremely well. As such it is a great idea to have it developed for various Forex applications.

You can easily connect Excel Forex Trader directly onto your trading platform. When you connect the two, you will receive currency pair prices directly onto your Excel. You will then be able to use any Excel functions and formulas so as to develop and analyze charts and obtain useful information for your trades.

5. Market Sentiment

This is an excellent Forex trading tool that especially useful for Forex positional traders. Using the Market Sentiment, you will be able to easily access a trader's true position all on a single dashboard. This tool also enables you to find out the number of traders holding long positions as well as those holding short positions.

Market Sentiment can help you determine whether you want to enter a trade and additional information such as your chances of success should you trade against the market.

6. Correlation matrix

Anytime that you examine a couple of Forex trading strategies you should try not to deal in currencies with correlation levels that are similar. The term correlation which it comes to Forex trading refers to the relation between the price changes of a currency compared to its pair.

A correlation matrix enables traders to gain insights into currency pairs correlations that are mapped out over different time frames. This is an amazing tool especially for novice traders and beginners in general because it enables you to avoid putting your margins in currencies that should be perform in a similar manner.

Forex trading tools summary

The notifications provided by the various Forex trading tools may not necessarily free but are crucial for the success of your trading strategy. They provide important data and information that is essential for implementing a successful strategy.

For instance, you will be notified if the stop-loss level or take-profit level is attained. The notifications provided by Forex tools are important for numerous traders especially those who may not be in possession of charts when they are needed. There are plenty of other tools available. They serve different purposes and are applied whenever a situation demands it.

More about Forex Trading Tools

Forex volatility tool:

This is a trading tool used by Forex traders and indicates the movement of a currency pair. Sometimes traders may be interested in the average movement over a period of thirty days. The volatility tool can narrow down the results to a brief period of the day. The information is sufficient to let you know how volatile a currency pair was during a certain period or day of the week and how the volatility changed with time. Volatility tools do not indicate the direction that a trade is heading but can inform a trader the magnitude of price movement.

Forex position summary tools

As a trader, you can sometimes receive an updated summary of your positions from your broker. This summary basically lets you know the position of other traders in the market. You can receive a summary showing 40% of clients are long on the USD/EUR while 60% are short on the same pair. This information on its own is not really helpful. What is more important is the change with time of the ratios. When the price moves, it will be possible to get deep insights on future price movements.

There are some tools that provide both historical position rations as well as currency position schools. These are extremely important if you wish to view the position ratios have indicated price direction change. For example, a price reversal can be deduced should current positions close in on historic levels.

Technical Indicators

Forex traders have a wide choice of tools to choose for their trading charts. These technical indicators include moving averages, RSI and even the MACD. Other less common ones include the TTM Trend, the envelopes, and the zigzag.

It is possible to customize the zigzag so that it indicates the percentage movement of the price and this can point to market tendencies of the price action. For instance, zigzag retracements often indicate that currencies basically retrace close to 56% of a trend then pulling back before proceeding in the same direction. Such a pattern can easily be picked out by a trader who will then fine tune the location and timing until a proper entry and exit point is identified.

Envelopes generally consist of three parallel lines that appear just above the price action. The line in the middle is the moving average. The envelope is generally used to provide an outlook on the possible trend direction and changes and also whether we have a weak or strong trend. If the price touches the top of the three lines then this means the trend is headed upwards. We can also adjust the moving average so that it behaves as either resistance or support.

We also have the TTM Trend which is a useful technical indicator. It tends to change the price bar colors on the chart. The changes in color will depend on the direction of the short term momentum. The bars will turn to a blue color when the trend heads upwards and red when the trend begins a downward movement.

In summary, technical indicators are not just the major ones like the moving averages. They are simply tools that can provide traders with information from other sources of information such as statistics and price formations. They can be used in combination to make them more effective. Remember that you do not have to use all these indicators when trading. Simply practice using a demo platform how to use them and then find the ones that work best for you.

Chapter 6: Preparations Prior to Market Entry

Building a trading plan is by far the single most important aspect of your success as a Forex trader. You absolutely have to take time and plan your trades from start to conclusion. All too often traders will enter a trade without a clear plan or vision. They believe that a particular trade is a winning one and they fear losing out. Such traders jump into a trade and start making profit. However, once the tide turns, they turn around and try again. This will lead to huge losses and profitability might be missed simply because there was no pre-trade planning.

It is crucial that you treat trading as a business and not a side gig or hobby. This way, you will take it more seriously and will have a better chance of success. If you have no idea what a trading plan or how it looks like, then it is better to learn as it is among the most crucial aspect of your trading life and success.

Forex Trading Considerations

As a trader, you need to understand that the key to success is actually emotional discipline and not intelligence. If the main ingredient was intelligence, then there would be a lot more people out there trading and making money. Even before you begin trading, think about the reasons why you are a Forex trader? What are your desires, ambitions, or aspirations? Are you seeking financial freedom or to be your own boss? Do you want to establish an additional source of income? Once you answer these questions, then you will be able to determine your motivation. It is this motivation that will keep you going from day to day, month to month and even for years to come. You need to keep in mind that trading Forex can be a fulltime job and is never a gamble. You can actually make money.

Have Realistic Trading Goals

As a trader, you need to think realistically about your goals and how you will go about achieving them. For instance, you cannot, as a trader, expect to earn a living trading Forex with an initial of $50, $500, or even $2000. With goals that are realistic, you will be able to set targets and meet them, feel motivated and keep going. Realistic goals also enable you to abide by risk management and money management rules.

Here are some realistic goals that you can set for yourself.

- Always have a trade strategy
- Trade according to your strategy
- Be consistently profitable after 12 months
- Ensure capital growth by 3% each month

What type of trader are you?

You need to determine what type of trader you are. There are different kinds of Forex traders. The type of trader you aspire to be is mostly related to your persona as well as the time you have to dedicate to your trades. Forex trading essentially occurs in timeframes. You need to determine the trading timeframe that suits you best. Here is a look at the different types of traders.

1. Scalper:

A scalper is basically a trader who prefers trading the lowest timeframes. Such traders do not want to wait for long hours for their trades. They enjoy speedy setups and enjoy a lot of time with the charts each day. A scalper searches for the lowest spreads within a currency pairs and often opts for the business times of the day for any major Forex currency pairs.

2. Day Trader

Most Forex traders are day traders. And many aspiring traders often envision themselves as day traders. Such traders don't enjoy scalping and they consider it to be nerve wracking. They are also not happy leaving trades open for lengthy periods of time. Day traders have plenty of time in their hands throughout the day and can spare moments to find trade setups and keep observing and monitoring them throughout the day. A day job is basically

3. Position Trader

A position trader is a Forex trader that enters a trade then finds and holds a position for a long while. This could be for weeks at a time and sometimes even for months. Therefore, they always base their trades, decisions, and moves on the fundamentals of a currency rather than technical analysis like other traders do. Such a trader needs to be very patient and must be able to predict the activity of the market within a month or longer. Such traders work with large stop losses mostly because of big market swings. They also need substantial capital amounts to affect their trades.

4. Swing Traders

A swing trader is a Forex trader who is happy to leave his or her trades open for a couple of days. Such a trader generally follows market swings in the correct direction. Swing trades often plan their trades intricately and prefer to focus on only a couple of trades at a time. These particular types of trades are suitable for people who do not have much time for their trades but are patient and willing to wait for lengthy periods of time for their trades to work right. Patience is a virtue for swing traders so keep that in mind. They also need to be disciplined enough not to exit a trade should the market move against them. An impatient trader would feel compelled to intervene, stop a trade, and possibly start a new one.

Determine the Kind of Trader you are

Part of your trading plan needs to contain your preferred type of Forex trade. When you eventually make the decision, make sure to write it down as part of your larger trading plan. There are a couple of things that will basically determine the kind of trader you are going to eventually become. These include your trading strategy.

Ideally, your trading strategy should define a couple of things including how you plan, select, open, manage, and eventually exit a trade. It is very likely that you have an idea on how you accomplish each step but it needs to be written down as part of your strategy. For instance, how do you choose your trades? What are the determining factors or essential ingredients?

Here are some of the essential ingredients that constitute a good trading strategy.

- Do you have a trading setup? Your trading setup should include things such as technical and fundamental indicators as well as trading timeframe.
- Do you have any established rules?
- Are there any exit tools?
- How are stop loss and take profit strategies determined?
- Will you use a trailing stop?
- Are there conditions that would compel you to quit a trade early?

What about Risk Management?

One of the most essential aspects of Forex trade and trading in general is risk management. This refers to the percentage of your trading capital that you are willing to risk in any trade. It also points to the risk: reward ratio. As a trader, you may be wondering how much of your capital you should be willing to risk. The answer basically should be not more than 2%. Therefore, anytime you want to come up with a trading strategy, always think about risk management. Risk management is always considered using the risk: reward ratio or the 2% maximum risk allowed.

Always Keep a Trading Journal

Another important aspect of trade planning is keeping or maintaining a trade journal. A trading journal is simply a logbook where you record all your trades. You should endeavor to make this as routine as possible. This is an excellent way of turning you into a profitable trader within a very short period. A journal allows you to take and record notes so that you note what great things happen and any lessons that need to be learned. It is important to keep a trading journal because;

- It allows you to record notes of your emotions and sentiments while trading. For instance, if you thought you were losing but ended up winning then you should not this down.
- A journal provides a reliable record of all your activity. This historic record enables you to conduct an analysis of previous trades so that you can determine what you did well and where you went wrong.
- It also enables you to confirm whether or not you followed the trading strategy that you had set out for yourself. If there were any discrepancies or failures, then these will become visible to you.

Summary of a Good Trading Plan

Here is a summary of the proper steps you need to take to come up with a suitable trading plan.

- Take into consideration your motivation for Forex trade

- Work within realistic goals so that you attain them
- Discover the kind of trader that you are
- Use a template to write down your trading plan
- Always have a risk management plan
- Ensure that you keep a trading journal

How to Make a Reliable Trading Plan

We have already determined that a Forex trading plan is essential for a successful trading strategy. Any plan that you come up with should be written in stone which means it should not change. However, it can be subjected to a review once the trading day is over or after the market has closed. Your plan can be adjusted as market conditions change and changed as your skills get better. Avoid using someone else's plan and come up with your own.

Asses your skill set

You need to determine whether you are ready to trade or not. If you have a system then you should test it until you have confidence that it works. You need to be like the professionals who trade the markets confidently. They move in and take profits from traders who have no plans and keep making expensive errors.

Have a check list and a routine

Any good trading plan should consist of a routine in trading activities. It is important to have a pre-determined routine so that you do not end up running around confused and out of focus. With the routine you will also need discipline. Also, you should choose the most obvious market setups whenever you can so that you pick up any easy trades. You can in fact formulate your entire trading plan and make it a check list. Having a smooth format that enables you to determine if a trade setup is worth it is absolutely important.

Trade Preparation

Make sure that you carefully determine the program and trading system that you will use. If you intend to use signals, then ensure that these are easily visible and can be detected clearly with a clear auditory or visual signal.

Come up with clear exit rules

A lot of traders often focus more on finding buy signals. 90% of their attention is spent looking for entry points and so on. However, they pay very little attention to the appropriate points of exit. Often, traders will not sell when they are down as they are unwilling to take a loss. To make it as a successful trader, you will need to overcome such concerns. A lot of professional traders lose more trades than they win but because of their money management and exit rules, they still end up making a profit.

Therefore, always find out your exit points before you enter a trade. Each trade has at least two exit points. Write down your stop loss points and do not count on mental notes. Also, ensure that each trade has a profit target. Once you hit this target you should collect some of your profits and then move your stop loss position to break even. Also, do not risk losing more than the percentage that you initially set.

Prepare yourself mentally

It is extremely important that you prepare yourself for the day ahead. You will need a clear head and focus. A good trader always has to be up to the challenge. Experienced traders will tell you that it is better to take the day off and not trade at all if you are psychologically and emotionally unprepared. Otherwise you will simply not be able to participate fully in any trade and you will not only lose huge amounts of money but will worsen your mental situation.

It is easy to be mentally unprepared when you are angry, distracted, or preoccupied with other thoughts. As a trader, you may want to have a mantra that you repeat regularly, probably once each day. Such a mantra should put you mentally at ease and into the trading zone. Also, avoid distractions within your trading area. Trading is business and distractions can cost you in a huge way.

Do both your homework and due diligence

It is important that every morning, just before your trades begin, you should become acquainted with the goings on around the world. What is the situation at the markets? Are overseas markets up or down? Is there any company about to release its earnings report? Most traders prefer to wait for the release of such reports before making any major moves. This is a much better approach than taking unnecessary risks. You can use index futures to gauge the mood of the market right before the markets open.

Come up with clear entry rules

Just like with the exit, you need to define and set clear entry rules. These rules will define how you enter a particular trade. It could be something like; if I have a signal B which fires and indicators show minimum target about 3 times larger than the stop loss and I am at support, then purchase Y contracts or X shares.

The system you use needs to be sufficiently complex to handle instructions effectively yet flexible enough to manage any snap decisions. For instance, if you have a total of 15 conditions that need to be fulfilled while most are subjective, then it may be challenging if not impossible to actually trade. It is worth noting that computers make much better traders compared to humans.

This is probably the reason why half of all trades on the New York Stock Exchange are executed by computer software and not people. Computers carry no emotions when trading. They simply follow a program set by a trader. When conditions are met, then they enter a trade. Should the trade proceed in the wrong direction, then they exit. But should a trade become profitable then the computer will take profits and exit. All decisions are based on probabilities and devoid of emotions and irrational thinking.

Post trade post-mortem

It is advisable to conduct a post-mortem of each trade. While adding up the profits and working out any losses is important, understanding why is ten times more important. Have a trading journal where you write all your conclusions so that you learn, improve, and remember.

Summary

It is important to gain sufficient skill before embarking on Forex trading. There is never a guarantee that any trade will make money. However, your chances as a trader will improve drastically if you are sufficiently skilled and have a system that can assist you win. All professional traders choose trades where the odds favor them otherwise they wouldn't trade. However, during trades, they allow their profits to ride a winning trade and cut their losses short. This can result in some losses but they will emerge winners overall.

Many traders who do not make money often do not trade the way that the pros do but instead do the exact opposite. Learning and improving skills should be one of your hallmarks. Also, as a trader, you need to treat your Forex trading as a fulltime job, part time job, or a business. It is never a gamble or a game where you depend on luck. This way, you will take is seriously enough and aim to make rather than lose money. While no trade is ever guaranteed, it is crucial that you have a suitable plan so that you have much better chances of winning and making a consistent profit.

Chapter 7: Forex Trading, Charts and Practice

There are several ways for Forex traders to enter the market. These include quantitative analysis, fundamental analysis as well as technical analysis. All the methods help Forex traders determine the direction or movement of Forex currencies.

Some traders may choose to use direct information such as events in the news, policies, economic variables, government policies, and things of that nature. Others prefer to use Forex trading charts together with other indicators. These, when used in combination, provide sufficient information that can guide a Forex trader to make appropriate decisions.

Regardless of your preferred trading method, you will actually need to learn how to read Forex charts. It is best to have a good grasp of the basics as well so that you eventually become a great Forex trader. Basically, you must learn how to crawl before you can walk.

What is a Forex chart?

A Forex chart is simply a chart that contains historical information on currency exchange rates. Using these charts, a trader will obtain information that they need to conduct technical analysis in relation to a specific currency pair. In short, a Forex chart is a graphical representation of the exchange rate between two currencies.

You are likely to come across Forex charts on most Forex platforms provided by respective brokers. Brokers often provide these to clients who have open and funded accounts.

If you examine a Forex chart closely, you will observe how the exchange rate of a particular currency pair has been changing over a period of time. The reason why these charts are important is because past financial events are great indicators of future events. Financial instruments such as currencies have been known to follow similar cycles and paths throughout history.

Forex chart timeframes

The amount of time indicated on a Forex chart depends on the exact timeframe that you want. Most of them however are set based on the one day timeframe by default. Therefore, a single point on the chart represents a single day's trading information. This is not fixed and can be changed to provide whatever timeframe you prefer.

Technical analysis

The information obtained from the charts will be used for technical analysis. The term technical analysis simply means reviewing past market analysis and prices with the use of technical indicators in order to foretell the future. Technical analysis helps foretell future market events and short-term movements.

According to Forex traders, price movements in the short term are caused by demand and supply forces. When charting in order to predict future price movement, you will need to use charting software. You will also need to choose from numerous technical indicators such as moving averages and so on. As a new trader, you should try out a couple of brokers to find out what their charts offer before choosing one.

Type of Forex charts

There are a couple of Forex chart types. The most common are the bar chart, line chart and candlestick chart. Most traders prefer the candlestick and there is a reason why. Candlestick charts contain a lot more information compared to the line and bar charts. This information is actually four times that produced by the line and bar graphs. It includes low and high prices, as well as closing and opening prices. This extra information gives you the advantage of knowing the price movement over a given period of time.

Forex indicators

We use currency charts to enables to better study and analyze market behavior and also determine currency movement for the future. For this to be implemented successfully, traders need to use additional indicators. There are numerous such indicators available. Most Forex traders use only some of the most crucial ones. These are mentioned below.

1. Bollinger bands: These are volatility lines that are located or aligned next to moving averages.

2. RSI – Relative Strength Index: This is a momentum indicator and shows the velocity and direction of price movements.

3. SMA – Simple Moving Average: This is one of the most popular indicators used by Forex traders. Together with other moving averages, they are mostly used to level out fluctuations in price over a specific period in time. They provide traders with a better visualization in regards to the price movement and direction.

Practice before Live Trading

It is extremely important that you learn how to use the Forex trading platform and how to make use of all the features available. The good news is that most brokers and all other platforms do provide demo accounts. Using these demo accounts, you can invest virtual money then apply a trading strategy and see how well you can implement one. Having the ability to test your skills and try out different strategies is an excellent way to get started. Once you get an understanding of how Forex works, you will simply need to open a demo account and begin implementing different strategies. With time, you will eventually learn how to trade Forex, how to interpret and apply your analysis and so much more.

Most major brokers provide customers and potential clients with a free demo platform that they can download and use. This is recommended before any client begins trading because familiarity with a platform makes trading easier. There are certain things that you should be on the lookout for even as you learn how to trade and apply different strategies.

Paper Trading

The term paper trading originated from the stock markets. Years ago, some traders wanted to practice trading before eventually trading live. These traders would take pieces of paper and then follow the market movements as they practiced trading.

Markets attract new traders all the time. Many of them are wary about losing their money and hesitant about entering the market directly. Many would rather learn the ropes first, practice trading, and once they feel confident enough, they'd enter the market. Paper trading is a common form of practice prior to entering the markets.

Trading has some level of risk involved. This is why it is important that you learn how to trade in order not to lose money. Different platforms provide different tools to their clients. These include demo platforms for practice. Paper trading is not as popular today as it used to be before. Since things went digital some years back, paper trading is sometimes referred to as trading a demo account.

Through the years, stock markets and Forex markets have let novice traders and beginners trade on their markets without actually putting any money at risk. As such, traders can enter trades confidently and practice their trading skills. They get opportunities to try out their skills and test their strategies. These are awesome cost free opportunities to try out different strategies and find out the ones that work best.

Modern and advanced technologies allow investors and traders to practice from any location they may be and at the time of their choosing. As such, traders gain useful opportunities to work on their skills and implement strategies so they know how different strategies perform when implemented under different market conditions. Such traders gain a unique advantage over other traders elsewhere because of the chance to paper trade.

Paper trading on the digital platform also enables traders to become fully conversant of different parameters and features available to them. They are also able to easily and freely navigate across trading platforms with ease. Today's trading platforms are versatile and robust and come with numerous tools and different features. Gaining as much experience as possible using these features and tools is crucial for successful trading on the markets eventually.

Benefits of paper trading

There are some obvious benefits of paper trading for all traders but especially novice traders and beginners. One of the top advantages of paper trading is that traders are able to trade without risking any capital. The thought of trading without risks enables traders, especially beginners, to gain sufficient practice and hone their skills.

More experienced traders also use paper trading when trying out new channels or testing a new strategy. By using paper trading, they are able to try out these new strategies and channels without worrying about losing money. Traders also get to learn the Forex market much better and gain a better understanding the kind of trader that they are. Paper trading therefore plays a useful role in the world of Forex trading.

Today paper trading is accomplished digitally. This means that traders have to open digital accounts and trade using a digital demo account. A demo account receives virtual money which can be spent trading on the virtual platform. All you will have to do is implement a particular strategy by opening positions and funding them. Demo accounts operate exactly like real Forex accounts including the features that they come with. In essence, traders at all levels get to enjoy stress free trading on a platform that is very similar to the real one.

Users of demo accounts they also have the benefit of learning from their mistakes. We all make mistakes and learning from them is the best that we can do. Therefore, demo accounts which are modern day paper traders are important in a number of ways. However, there are a couple of disadvantages.

Disadvantages of paper trading

There are some downsides to paper trading. One of these is euphoric trading. Since there are no losses to incur traders can get careless and trade without a care. Traders end up taking major risks with their trades since there is no money at risk. In reality, traders never make highly risky trades for fear of incurring major losses. Paper trading causes traders to lower their guard and risk most of their funds.

Money lost on the demo platform is inconsequential and never taken too seriously. This is a major challenge because it introduces complacency. Traders tend to place trades on their demo accounts that they wouldn't dare on the real platform using real money.

Also, funds are crucial when it comes to Forex traders. We need to be careful with our trading capital at all times. Unfortunately, demo platforms or paper trading cause us to be careless and traders may end up losing large sums on the live platform if they are not careful. Some traders also fail to act as thought the market was a real one. This way, they will not always follow the markets and their trading approach may be affected.

In some instanced, demo accounts experience delayed data. Basically the data available is never actually fresh but old and outdated. Some platforms use fake data while others introduce delays. The main aim of paper trading is to sharpen a trader's skills and prepare them for the real platform. Fake or delayed data does not strongly support this aim. Traders sometimes refer to paper trading as "Trading with paper money or monopoly money". This creates an attitude that belittles trading altogether.

Is paper trading worth your time?

According to experts, paper trading is definitely recommended. It provides an excellent platform for traders to hone their skills and practice trading without worrying about incurring losses. However, traders should treat paper trading with the seriousness it deserves.

If done well and taken seriously, then paper trading will enable traders to try out their strategies, make use of different features and come up with the best strategy possible. Practice definitely makes perfect so novice traders who spend a lot of time paper trading will improve their skills, understand the workings and functions of the trading platform and much more.

Also, a trading simulator is the most suitable trading tool that learners need. Such a platform will help to transform them from amateur traders and novices into profitable traders in just a couple of weeks. You also get to learn your level of risk, things such as trading discipline, and the type of trader that you are. Therefore, when the opportunity of trading risk-free on a demo platform arises, you should seize it and practice as often as possible. This way, you will eventually become an excellent trader who is consistently profitable.

Forex Trading Platforms

There are plenty of Forex trading platforms out there. Most of these have plenty of similar features and even appearance. There are some common ones that you are likely to come across. These platforms include the MT4 and MT5 which are abbreviations for Meta Trade 4 and Meta Trade 5. These two are currently the most popular. Some traders do not offer demo platforms at all. You have to sign up and open an account in order to access one.

Platforms are generally different but most of the functions available are pretty similar across the board. The most common features are technical analysis tools, charts, drawing tools, news feed, Forex quotes, trade history as well as buttons that enable purchase and sale of stocks.

There are platforms that have a lot more features than your average broker provides. You are likely to come across certain economic and fundamental analysis tools which are not found on other platforms. These are extremely useful to traders seeking long-term ventures. However, short-term traders can thrive without these additional tools.

On the trading platform you are also likely to come across shortcut features that help to save you time as you execute trades. You will also notice additional features such as buttons that provide access to information on current trades, latest news, and so much more.

Place virtual or demo orders

Now that you have a better understanding about Forex trading platforms, it is now time to place your first order. Experts advise beginners and novice traders to place at least 50 different trades on a platform just to gain the necessary experience. This way, you will be sure that you have sufficient trading experience in order to go live and trade using real money. Before you trade live, there are a couple of questions that you should ask yourself. These questions include;

- Do I know how to set up a stop order?
- What is the procedure of setting up a limit order?

- Is it possible to have a stop order and limit order for the same trade?
- How large are the lot sizes that I can trade? (e.g. 1,000 units)
- Is it possible to mix and match different lot sizes?
- Am I able to phone the deal room should my internet slow down?

You should be able to answer all the above questions before trading using real money. Otherwise you will probably be risking your money because your skills may not be up to par.

When you want to purchase a currency pair, you need to get to the chart and click directly on the prices. To purchase Forex pairs, you will view some quotes featuring your preferred currency pair. There is the ask portion of the order and the bid part. You should click on the ask part of you wish to purchase and bid if you wish to sell.

There are platforms that let you select the limit order or market order once the quote window appears. Some others make it mandatory to make a choice beforehand. Once you decide on the currency pair and price, you should then choose volumes. This simply means the quantity of trades you wish to enter. Once the volume is determined, you should determine and enter both the stop-loss level as well as the profit-take level. These are the points during trading where you exit once you start taking losses and where you collect profits and exit a trade respectively.

You will notice that there are different kinds of orders such as pending orders and market orders. Should you want to purchase or sell at indicated price levels, then you should select the market price. If you wish to sell or buy at different price levels then choose the pending level. Once you have filled out the form completely, you should submit it. This will complete the order placing process and the order will be received.

Treat the demo like real trading

Once you begin trading on the demo account, you should first focus on mastering the different functions and other trading basics. Checkout your different strategies and implement them one by one as best as you can. This way, you will be able to identify the one that you like best.

There are different kinds of strategies including long-term trading with less leverage, short-term momentum traders, scrappers, day traders, and so on. It is only through practice that you will be able to find the ideal strategy for you. Even then, demo trading is simply Forex trading practice and not actual trading. You should apply yourself to these demo trades the best way you can. This means treating trades with seriousness and care.

Sometimes you may incur huge losses on your demo trades. You may not feel anything and will simply remain calm because you haven't actually lost anything. However, in real life, even small losses may jolt you awake. If you want to benefit from demo Forex trading, then you should treat the trading process as if it were real. As an example, you should trade with $5,000 and not $50,000 if you intend to fund your real account with only $5,000.

Prepare to Enter the Forex Market
Chapter 8: Essential Preparations for Live Trading

Forex traders, especially beginners, need to learn about the steps necessary for profitable trading. Achieving long term success trading profitably is a dream that many have but only a few can achieve. Fortunately there are steps that you can take that will ensure you become a successful, long term, profitable trader. Here is a look at some of the essential steps that will lead you to successful trades.

1. Choose the Right Broker

When you feel totally ready to begin trading Forex currencies, then you should first embark on identifying a fair, trustworthy, and reliable Forex broker. You may be a great trader but without a reliable and trustworthy broker, you will not be as successful as you should.

You may have an idea of what a Forex broker is but it is important that we define who he is so that you have no doubt. A Forex broker can be defined as a company or firm that provides traders like you with access to a trading platform. As a trader, you need this platform so as to gain direct access to the Forex Market. Brokers are usually compensated via the bid-ask spreads of a given Forex currency pair.

The first step you should take is search for reviews of the broker and find out what other traders think about him, his platform and services. Conducting due diligence is a must for any serious trader. You also need to check out the trading platform to find out if it matches your needs. Different traders have different needs when it comes to Forex trading so finding a right match is crucial.

Most Forex brokers will allow traders, who are possible clients, a chance to try out their platforms and test their services. They do this by offering a demo account. This provides traders with an excellent opportunity to try and understand how the system is like, how it functions and operates. As a trader, you need to try out as many platforms as possible so that you find one that you are quite happy and content with.

The Forex market operates 24 hours a day and sees a daily turnover in excess of $4 trillion. This makes it the world's largest financial market. as a trader, you will need some help navigating this market so your broker should be able to assist you as you trade on their platform.

1. Check for regulatory compliance

Most reputable Forex brokers are members of the NFA or National Futures Association and also registered with the US government as a commission merchant via the US Commodity Futures Trading Commission.

The NFA is an industry-wide body and self-regulating organization that covers the entire futures market in the USA. On the other hand, the CTFC is an independent government body that regulates the options markets and commodities futures markets in America. Their aim is basically to protect the public as well as market users from manipulation.

A professionally looking website belonging to a Forex trader does not in any way guarantee that the broker is registered or regulated. Most of them will state that they are registered with the authorities and will display their registration details. You should never deposit your precious trading capital onto just any trading platform. Deal only with Forex brokers that are properly licensed and duly registered.

2. Apply Proper Customer Service

Traders can access Forex markets at any time of day or night because the markets are accessible 24-

hours each day. Your chosen broker should be available to provide you with essential services all the time. It should also be pretty simple to be able to access someone on phone for help. While chat-based service will do most of the time, there are instances when speaking to a real person will be of great assistance. Before signing up to any platform, consider making a quick call to customer service just so you get a feel of the quality of the customer service that they offer.

3. Study the Currency Pairs Available

There are plenty of different currency pairs and even individual currencies out there. However, when it comes to Forex trading, only a couple of pairs are of any major importance. Some of the most useful Forex pairs include EUR/USD, GBP/USD, USD/CHF, and USD/JPY. Some top Forex brokers might offer a wider choice that may include the Chinese Yuan, the Hong Kong dollar, Australian dollar and so on. Always check out the list and ensure that the currency pairs you are interested in are available.

4. Take a Closer look at the Trading Portal

As a trader, you are connected directly to the Forex markets via the portal. It is therefore absolutely imperative that the portal is visually presentable and simple to use. You will be using this platform to practically carry out all the operations of your trades. Ensuring that it is in excellent working condition, easy to use, and reliable is something you must do. A good trading platform should come with essential buttons such as a simple sell or buy button. It should also come with an emergency button that allows traders to close all their open positions.

If the platform is poorly designed, then it will put your trades at huge risks. For instance, you could go short instead of long, or accidentally add to a given position instead of closing, and so on. Such mistakes will not only cost you money but also emotionally distressing. There are excellent options out there such as the Meta Trader which is among the most popular options among Forex traders.

While there is no perfect Forex broker in the world, identifying an excellent platform will allow you to focus more on your trades and technical analysis. You will then have more time to focus on developing appropriate trade strategies.

The Essential Features of Online Forex Brokers

Every major Forex broker offers accounts with various features. These include some of the following.

1. Leverage and margin

As a trader, you will have access to a wide range of leverage amounts. These amounts will really depend on your Forex broker. Leverage could be 50:1, 100:1 and so on. The term leverage simply refers to a loan that you can access if you are a margin account holder. If you are an account holder and your account has a capital of $1000, then a Forex broker offering leverage of 50:1 will allow you to hold a position worth $50,000.

Leverage does work in favor of a trader especially when holding a winning position. The reason is that such a position stands a great chance of being profitable and making money. However, caution is needed because if a trade starts heading in the wrong direction, then the potential for losses is huge and could wipe out a trader's account. Therefore, caution is imperative whenever leverage is sought.

2. Spreads and Commissions

Online Forex brokers make their money mostly from spreads and commissions. Some opt for commissions which charge traders a certain percentage for accessing their platform. Sometimes the broker will charge based on the difference between the bid and ask price of a currency pair. Most traders prefer not to charge a commission but instead prefer to charge or make a commission from spreads. Generally it is harder for a trader to make a profit on a wider spread. Common trading Forex pairs like the EUR/USD or GBP/USD have much tighter spreads compared to other pairs that may not be as tightly paired.

Forex brokers often offer first time traders or new clients a free amount which they can access and use to trade. Most Forex accounts are funded with very little money, sometimes as little as $50 or $100. However, this amount can greatly increase due to the offers and access to leverage power. This is among the reasons why Forex trading is so popular with first time traders. As a new trader with a new account, you will have the option of opening either a mini, standard, or micro account. Each account has a minimum deposit requirement so this is worth noting.

3. Ease of withdrawals and deposit

Generally all major Forex brokers have their own policies when it comes to depositing and withdrawing your money. They also have things such as a funding policy and so on. A good broker will enable a variety of payment options including use of credit cards, direct payments from bank accounts or ACH, use of bank checks, wire transfers and also use of online payment processors like PayPal and others.

Withdrawals from accounts are often processed via wire transfers or checks. Reputable brokers usually charge a processing fee during withdrawals. However, there is often no charge for making a deposit. You should check out these features before signing up with any broker.

Learn Proper Money Management Strategies

As a Forex trader, you will have to take risks with your capital. There is no strategy that is 100% profitable and even professional Forex traders lose money on some trades. The focus is always on the amount or percentage lost. Before entering any trade, you need to have a good strategy including the loss you are willing to incur before exiting a trade.

Most traders are willing to risk between 1% and 2% of their capital. Some are willing to get to 5%. However, the percentage you choose will largely depend on your risk appetite. There are a couple of things that you need to keep in mind though. When trading, the volumes could increase drastically and this could have an effect on your capital. You will need to be flexible with some of your money management techniques when the time calls for it. This way, you will avoid losing money on your trades.

Some of the essential money management techniques that apply here include setting up your stop loss strategy. You need to decide exactly where to locate this important feature. The stop loss feature can be adjusted based on the current situation in the market as well as its volatility. It is only after the stop loss process is complete that you will decide on the volumes of trade. Remember that money management is a crucial step and decisive part of any profitable trading strategy and should, therefore, not be overlooked but treated with the seriousness that it deserves.

Have the Right Trading Psychology

A successful trader has many admirable characteristics. These include the ability to determine stocks' direction and understanding a company's fundamentals. However, the single most crucial characteristic is the ability to exercise discipline and contain emotion.

What is Trading psychology?

One of the most significant aspects of trading is the psychological aspect. Traders are often jumping in and out of trades on very short notices. Most of the time traders have to make very quick decisions with immense ramifications. A certain degree of calmness and presence of mind is therefore required. Emotions should never be allowed to cloud a trader's judgment or cause them to deviate from established trading plans.

The area of Forex trading is quite high paced with numerous possibilities and just as many pitfalls. Most of the time traders feel like the odds are stacked against them. Anytime a trader receives news about a certain currency, it is not uncommon to get scared. Sometimes they overreact and feel compelled to end a trade and other irrational acts. By so doing, a Forex trader may prevent losses but will also lose out on any possible profits.

Understanding fear

Traders need to understand what fear. This is a natural reaction to what a person perceives as a threat. Traders need to face up to this fear and see how they can get rid of it. Conquering fear is never easy and it does take some time and practice but it is an essential aspect that needs to be tackled sooner rather than later. It is important for traders to isolate the single fear element, focus on it and try to isolate it as they trade. This is not as easy as it sounds but it works eventually.

Greed is your Worst Enemy

On Wall Street, traders have an adage that says, "Pigs get slaughtered". This saying simply means that any greedy Forex traders will eventually lose out. Such traders tend to cling to a winning position and try to earn as much money out of it as possible.

Overcoming this negative emotion is never easy. This is because greed is based on a positive instinct that you can do better. However, getting just a little more out of a trade can cause a lot of trouble. This is why it is advisable to learn to keep emotions in check, to have a suitable trading plan and to determine the profitability and any losses on any given trade.

Tips and Advice for Successful Forex Trading

Trading is more of an art than a science even though it is known for its ratios, charts, graphs, and numbers. Therefore, apart from learning the theory, you will need to hone your trading skills through regular practice and discipline. Keep doing self analysis and test your trading plans to see how effective they are. There are essentially a number of steps which, if adhered to, will ensure that you trade safely and also make great profits.

A lot of undisciplined and inexperienced traders have incurred large losses over the years. You do not want to be like them. If you can determine the important steps and tips that will keep you safe and earn you money, then you will definitely be successful.

Never 100% Successful

It is a fact that no trader is ever successful 100% of the time. Many lose some of their trades but then they win big on other trades. Successful Forex trading is possible and can happen. However, you should not expect a 100% win rate. As a trader, you should endeavor to match up to the behavior and personality of the Forex markets. This means you should align your thoughts and practices to align with the Forex market and how it works and not the other way around. This is an absolutely crucial point. You should NOT endeavor to bend the market so it becomes what you want it to be.

You can Succeed with 60% Wins or Lose with 80% Wins

Winning up to 80% of the trades you enter is absolutely phenomenal. A 0.8 win ratio is very respectable in the Forex world. However, you still lost

20% of the trades you entered which can be a little disappointing. Yet there are traders and trading systems that experience 60% wins or less. It is possible to be successful with only 45% wins.

Take the example of a trader who invests $1000 with the chance of winning $5000. Such a trader can afford to lose 4 trades because with just one win, he will emerge $1000 richer. This is how it is possible to emerge a winner with less than 50% wins.

On the other hand, consider the trader who invests $5000 to win only $1000. This is a risky set up and the trader cannot afford to lose. The losses will be too costly. While this is just a demonstration, it shows how it is possible to lose over 50% of your trades and still emerge a winner.

Reduce your Overall Risk during Trading

There are plenty of factors that determine the outcome of a trade. As your skill level increases so will your ability to spot lucrative trade setups. Trading can be simple but is never easy. As a trader you should endeavor to reduce your risks and exposure when trading in the foreign exchange markets. Here are some steps that you can take in order to keep yourself and your trades secure.

- **Start Trading with Small Amounts and Increase Organically**

One of the best tips that you can use is to start small. Do not load your account with a huge sum but try and start small. Use small amounts and low leverage. This is very important. You will be able to apply the skills you have learnt and focus on trades without the fear of making huge losses. If you are to grow your account, then ensure that you grow your capital amount organically. This means let the capital grow from the returns of your trades and not loading your account from other sources.

- **Timing is Key so learn to be Patient**

As a trader, you really need to learn patience because it is an essential ingredient for success. One of the most important acts should be your opening trade. This is a crucial trade so you should give it your best analysis. You should also assess all other potential trades in good time. Make sure that you correctly time your market entry because correct timing for this initial entry is crucial for success. For this you will need to apply all your skills and knowledge about market trends and charting techniques. You should also ensure that you understand the entire process so that you are absolutely sure of what you are doing.

- **Learn the Limits of a Position before Entering**

Every time you enter a trade, you must not only set your stop loss but also determine the maximum allowable loss that you are willing to take. The rules are pretty simple: Make sure you only risk money that you can afford o lose. Also, ensure that anytime you assess a position size and money required, there are sufficient funds for the trade. Avoid mixing cash meant for other projects with your trading capital.

You also need to set a total loss limit at the close of each month. If at any one time during the month you get to this limit, then trading should cease and you should wait for the following month. Also, should your losses consistently exceed your income, then you should probably cease trading and take a step back. Take time to reassess your strategies, revamp your technical skills, and trading fundamentals. Also, have a journal of all your trades so that you review them and take note of where it is that you are going wrong. Should you go back to trading and start making profits, put aside some funds just incase anything goes wrong. Such setbacks should be mitigated with the funds you set aside.

- **Remember to be Diligent and with your Trading Plan**

As a Forex trader, you will enjoy success when you eventually learn to balance hard work such as chart analysis with sound judgments and lots of patience. Too many traders often give up on their trades without giving them sufficient time to run their course. This is why a majority of first time traders and investors eventually give up and quit. To be a winner, you should learn patience, stick to your plan and do not quit.

How to determine the most Suitable Trading Strategy

There are many Forex traders out there who spend years implementing trading strategies that do not match them. This can be disastrous because the chances of success are very low. It is important to make some considerations before embarking on trading using a particular strategy. Here are some useful points that you should consider. When you take these points into consideration, then you are likely to save yourself a lot of hurt, pain, time, effort, and money.

1. Determine if you Want a Regular Income or Grow Wealth

First let us understand the difference between earning an income from trade and growing wealth. If you trade Forex to earn an income, then you probably target to earn a certain amount each month for your own personal use. However, when you want to grow wealth, you aim to grow your amount by a certain percentage each year.

Trading for an income

If you want to trade Forex in order to earn a monthly or weekly income, then you need to identify trades that occur within a short period of time. It also means that you should spend more hours on the trading platform. Some of the options you have regarding trade strategies include short term swing trading, day trading, and scalping.

Trading to grow wealth

You can choose to have fewer trading options when you want to grow your wealth. This essentially allows you to spend fewer hours on the trading platform by choosing trades with higher timeframes. Some of the trading options you can choose include position trading and swing trading.

2. Determine the Amount of Time you have

You need to decide how much time you can dedicate to Forex trading each day and each week. People with a fulltime job and those who cannot put in 12-hour days should consider Forex strategies that do not require a lot of time investment. These including position trading and swing trading.

Forex trade strategies like scalping, day trading and all other short term trading strategies are for traders with all the time in the world. Therefore, choose any of these strategies if you enjoy them.

3. Find out if a Particular Strategy Suits you

There are a good number of Forex trading strategies out there. All these can be split into two distinct categories. These are high win strategies with low reward: risk ratios and the low win rate with high reward: risk ratio.

You need to determine which of these two approaches suits you best. Apparently, they can both make you money as they are both profitable. Therefore, you need to determine which of these two categories you are more comfortable with.

Do you wish to take huge risks for high returns or are you comfortable playing it safe with low risk trades? Swing trading, for instance, has a high chance for success but with low returns. On the other hand, position trading has lower win rates with much larger gains.

Summary

In short therefore, we can conclude the following:

Swing trading: This strategy can be used for wealth creation or income generation. It is suitable for traders who can only spare a couple of hours each day to trade.

Day trading: This strategy is more popular with traders seeking to generate a regular income. It requires a Forex trader who has time on their hands and can spend long stretches of time in front of a screen.

Position trading: This is more of a wealth building strategy and is best suited for traders who do not have a lot of time on their hands. Such people often have another job or occupation elsewhere.

Before you embark on learning about any of these Forex trading strategies, you should first make the following determinations.

- What trading goals do you have?
- How much time do you have available?
- Does a particular strategy or approach suit your personality?

Only when you are able to address these concerns should you then proceed to start trading.

Conclusion

Thank for making it through to the end of this book, let's hope it was informative and able to provide you with all of the tools you need to achieve your goals whatever they may be.

The next step is to begin practicing the various skills and techniques you have learnt. Remember that trading is not theoretical but practical. As such, you need to get onto a platform and begin applying your knowledge. No Forex trader has ever enjoyed success by simply reading Forex topics widely. Gaining knowledge and information is advisable and you should do that. However, of greater importance is applying this knowledge, honing your trading skills, learning the ropes, and simply becoming a better trader each and every day.

As a rule of thumb, you should not begin trading until you have a clear understanding of how Forex trading works. There are lots of important things involved including technical and fundamental analysis, reading charts and interpreting the direction and all the various strategies. Only after plenty of practice over a number of weeks should you then begin to trade. When you feel ready and comfortable on the trading platform, then you can place your first trade and see how it goes.

Remember that there is a lot that makes a great trader. For instance, you need to be disciplined and have your emotions in check. These are essential ingredients for success. Basically, if you apply all the things expressed in this book, then you should become a successful Forex trader in time.

Finally, if you found this book useful in anyway, a review on Amazon is always appreciated!

Printed in Great Britain
by Amazon